CHANGING COURSE

CHANGING COURSE

Civil Rights at the Crossroads

CLINT BOLICK

Transaction Books
New Brunswick (U.S.A.) and Oxford (U.K.)

Library of Congress Catalog Number: 87-17317
ISBN: 0-88738-179-0
Printed in the United States of America

Library of Congress Cataloging in Publication Data

Bolick, Clint.
  Changing course: civil rights at the crossroads / Clint Bolick.
  p.   cm.
ISBN 0-88738-179-0
  1. Civil rights—United States.   I. Title.
JC599.U5B557   1987
323.4′0973—dc19   87-17317

This book was written by the author in his private capacity. No official support or endorsement of the U.S. Department of Justice, Equal Employment Opportunity Commission, or any other agency of the U.S. Government is intended or should be inferred.

FOR EVAN DREW,
the next generation

Contents

Acknowledgments — ix

Introduction — xi

Part I   The Rise and Fall of Civil Rights in America — 1

Introduction to Part I — 3

1. Origins of the Quest — 5

2. Abolitionism: The Quest for Freedom — 13

3. The Triumph of Opportunity — 31

4. The Quest Abandoned — 53

Part II   Recharting the Course of Civil Rights — 79

Introduction to Part II — 81

5. The Failed Agenda — 84

6. A New Civil Rights Strategy — 92

7. The Necessity of Judicial Action — 122

8. The Prognosis for Success — 142

Conclusion — 146

Index — 149

Acknowledgments

I am deeply indebted to the many individuals who assisted me in writing this book. I am particularly grateful to Chairman Clarence Thomas and Vice Chairman Ricky Silberman of the Equal Employment Opportunity Commission (EEOC), whose sensitivity and insights into civil rights provided enormous inspiration to me.

Special thanks also to Irving Louis Horowitz and Scott Bramson of Transaction Books for publishing this book; to the Cato Institute for sponsoring my research; to Brenda Vestal and Amy Alexander for producing the manuscript; to Diane Fredericks, Melinda Davison, and Cheryl Sarreals for research and technical assistance; to Chip Mellor of the Pacific Research Institute and Arthur Abel for their sage comments; to Willa Johnson for her inspiration and assistance; to my colleagues at the EEOC and Department of Justice for their support and good humor; and to my wife Joanne and son Evan for tolerating the myriad nights and weekends devoted to this endeavor.

Introduction

We have come a long way in the past two centuries in the realm of what we know as "civil rights." The transition from a society in which slavery was sanctioned and abetted by law to one in which all Americans share basic freedoms has not been an easy one. We are today still reminded of our often shameful past—and distance we have yet to travel—by such spectacles as the gang killings of blacks in Howard Beach, N.Y.; by the presence of the Ku Klux Klan at a civil rights rally in Forsyth County, Georgia; by the crude bigotry directed toward Asian entrepreneurs in Washington, D.C.; and, perhaps most vividly, by the ongoing outrage of apartheid in South Africa.

I acknowledge at the outset that I am not a veteran of the civil rights movement. The *Brown v. Board of Education* decision was already three years old when I was born. Images of the great struggles leading to the Civil Rights Act of 1964 lie at the periphery of my childhood memories.

My generation's historical detachment exacerbates the tremendous polarization that surrounds civil rights issues today. On one side, many proclaim the civil rights movement is over and must be replaced by an ambitious program to attain and exploit political power. On the other side is a backlash of resentment by those who feel victimized by "reverse discrimination." This malignant alienation threatens to destroy the nation's doctrinal commitment to civil rights and to spell a premature end to the civil rights movement.

This book is devoted to placing the current state of affairs in its historical perspective. Its thesis is that what we need to reverse the backsliding of the civil rights movement is an examination of the methods and principles that produced the movement's great triumphs, thus enabling true advocates of civil rights to restore consensus and move forward again.

To do so, we must begin with the tradition that binds us together, a tradition whose existence and persistence has been a unique feature of the American experience for two hundred years. The founders of the American experiment defined civil rights as natural rights enshrined in civil law. They stressed an absolute equality of rights, not only because they viewed all individuals as equal in the eyes of their Creator, but in order to safeguard the underlying fundamental rights: if rights are equal, the sanctity of one's own rights is dependent upon scrupulous respect for the rights of others.

The principle of the equality of fundamental rights animated the civil rights movement from the Declaration of Independence, to the abolition of slavery, to the guarantee of equal protection of the laws, to the demise of "Jim Crow" and the repudiation of "separate but equal"—from Thomas Paine, to William Lloyd Garrison, to Frederick Douglass, to Abraham Lincoln, to Booker T. Washington, to W.E.B. DuBois, to Martin Luther King. The legacy of the quest for civil rights in America is a steadfast commitment to the principle that distinctions in rights based on race, color, or national origin have no place in a rational, just society.

Tragically, a dramatic and fundamental reversal took place in the civil rights agenda during the past two decades, just as the movement was approaching its zenith. Many of those who today invoke the mantle of leadership have attempted to transform the very nature of civil rights from those basic freedoms we all share equally as Americans into special privileges for some and burdens for others, based solely on the same characteristics they once fought to render irrelevant. They have exchanged "color blindness" for color consciousness; equality of opportunity for forced equality in result; individual liberty for group reparations; civil rights for social engineering; justice for power. They have abandoned their role as statesmen and assumed the role of politicians; and, in so doing, they have tarnished the rich legacy they inherited. The civil rights mission has been cast adrift, its future agenda uncharted and its moral leadership unclaimed.

This book is about the rise and fall of the quest for civil rights in America. It traces the development of civil rights from their origins through their abandonment, and confronts the revised agenda of the contemporary civil rights establishment, the parody that masquerades as a civil rights movement today.

But that is not enough. Numerous critiques of this revised agenda already exist. What is lacking is a well-defined alternative designed to restore meaning and integrity to the quest for civil rights—a new strategy, translating the basic principles of civil rights into a dynamic program for action designed to confront the real civil rights issues we face today. And, of course, the will to implement it.

Without such an alternative, attacks on the revised agenda ring hollow. Abstract invocations of color-blindness and opposition to quotas and reverse discrimination are inadequate. The new strategy must recognize that many in our society have never experienced a truly equal opportunity to fully participate in the American system, and it must provide a clear blueprint to promote the vested interest in civil rights that we must all share in order to preserve them. It must be a *positive* strategy, predicated on the original premises underlying the civil rights vision, offering a viable alternative to the statism promoted by the purveyors of divisiveness and despair.

As in the past, the new civil rights strategy will necessarily transcend the limitations of "liberal" and "conservative," and must appeal to all who value individual dignity and autonomy. Specifically, the strategy should focus on eradicating what has historically constituted the greatest impediment to civil rights—government action that violates fundamental rights or discriminates on the basis of immutable characteristics. This focus has traditionally provided the civil rights movement with its greatest triumphs, and we must restore that emphasis today if we are to regain the momentum that has been reversed during the past two decades.

The principal contemporary deprivations of civil rights are not difficult to identify. In at least three areas, government policies disproportionately and unjustifiably frustrate civil rights and burden minorities and the poor, particularly poor blacks, and the agenda must provide thoughtful and principled solutions. First, we must propose to liberate the free enterprise system to provide the types of entry-level opportunities that have traditionally fostered upward mobility for countless individuals among the enterprising poor. We must challenge as violations of civil rights the pervasive barriers to entrepreneurial opportunities erected by every level of government. Second, we must expand educational opportunities beyond the narrow confines of the public educational monopoly that perpetuates poverty by stifling intellectual achievement. By opening education to free and vigorous competition from the private sector, thousands of poor and minority children who would otherwise be consigned to a bleak future can gain greater control over their lives. Third, we must deal with the vicious cycle of poverty that destroys individual pride and initiative—the system of enforced dependency that enslaves its victims in a manner more subtle yet no less debilitating than its predecessors. While much of the onus for escaping this cycle necessarily rests upon the resolve and ingenuity of its victims, a positive civil rights agenda must confront the government policies that reinforce the shackles that prevent an escape from poverty.

This book defines several specific objectives that can be implemented through vigorous and creative action in the legislative and judicial arenas, designed to make good on the promise of equal opportunity under the law that is the very cornerstone of civil rights. But the strategies presented here are far from exhaustive, and additional alternatives are limited only by the imaginations of their potential architects. Of far greater importance than any particular strategy presented in this book is the critical need to replenish the nature and spirit of the civil rights vision and to offer a viable and attractive alternative to the seductive enticement of equality without effort. Only then can we recapture the moral high ground and regain leadership in the fight for civil rights.

For those who would complain that a focus on principles is too abstract, too divorced from the practical problems facing the most disadvantaged in our society, I submit the problems confronting us today are precisely a consequence of abandoning fundamental principles. I believe a good dose of those principles will go far in restoring momentum to a civil rights movement that has been drifting aimlessly for a generation.

Twenty years ago, this nation was on the threshold of ensuring civil rights for all Americans. But instead of crossing that threshold, we began to turn back the clock to a bygone era in which opportunities were predicated not upon individual merit and ambition, but upon the most immutable, irrational characteristics. The time is now to rediscover our "first principles" and renew our quest for civil rights.

Part I

THE RISE AND FALL OF
CIVIL RIGHTS IN AMERICA

Introduction to Part I

It is at all times necessary ... that we frequently refresh our patriotism by reference to first principles. It is by tracing things to their origin that we learn to understand them: and it is by keeping that line and origin always in view that we never forget them.

—Thomas Paine, *Dissertation on First Principles of Government* (1775)

The quest for civil rights in America is well into its third century. But despite this history, perhaps less agreement exists today than at any time before over such seminal issues as the definition of civil rights, who they belong to, and whether they are relevant and important enough to justify the effort required to preserve and advance them. Little consensus or progress on the civil rights issues that confront us today is possible without addressing these threshold issues. Part I will address these issues as a necessary prerequisite to devising solutions to contemporary problems of civil rights.

To fully comprehend the tragic nature of the quagmire we face today and to equip ourselves to begin moving forward again, we must understand the historical context in which the quest for civil rights has developed. This development has progressed through three principal historical stages during which the underlying principles remained constant even while the goals of the movement evolved.

The movement's embryonic stage took place in the pre-Revolutionary era, during which the core principles of civil rights were articulated and refined. These principles furnished both the moral justification for revolution against Great Britain and the *raison d'etre* for the new government and culminated in the founding instruments of the American republic.

This stage was followed by the abolitionist period, during which the principles of the Revolution were marshalled against the most profound violation of civil rights—the institution of slavery. The abolitionist movement presaged the Civil War and inspired additional legal bulwarks for civil rights in the form of national legislation and constitutional amendments designed to resolve once and for all the questions that divided and wracked the conscience of America.

3

The third stage encompassed a century of further struggle, during which America was called upon to make good on the promise of equal opportunity. During this period, the civil rights movement surmounted enormous obstacles and produced a strong national consensus, finally producing a triumph of opportunity, marked by the Supreme Court's *Brown v. Board of Education* decision in 1954 and the Civil Rights Act a decade later. America was on the verge of making its civil rights vision a reality.

The common theme unifying each of these stages was a remarkable philosophical continuum, anchored to the original core principles underlying the concept of civil rights. This continuum allowed each successive stage of the movement to occupy the moral high ground and build upon the successes of its predecessors.

But apart from these core principles, which remained constant for more than two centuries, the quest for civil rights has not always been harmonious. Each stage has been followed by what A. Philip Randolph described in 1966 as a "crisis of victory"—a period of introspection and internal debate over the movement's future strategies and objectives. Fortunately, in the past, these crises have produced a strengthened resolve fortified by a renewed dedication to the unifying principles that animated the civil rights vision.

Today, however, America is in the throes of a crisis distinguished from previous crises by the movement's sudden and dramatic departure from the traditional principles of civil rights. Indeed, the present crisis is primarily one of identity. Until recently, civil rights were generally understood as those fundamental rights that are shared equally by all Americans—the rights to life, liberty, and property. So defined, they created a universally shared vested interest in civil rights, for even those who possessed little material wealth desired to preserve the system that would provide opportunities for them and their children. But during the past two decades, this consensus has eroded, and the definition of civil rights has become dependent upon one's vantage point. Those in whose name civil rights are today most frequently invoked interpret them as "rights" to particular outcomes such as economic subsistence and preferential treatment. Accordingly, those against whom they are invoked have come to associate civil rights with social engineering, parasitism, and even violence.

By recasting civil rights in this fashion, the movement has assumed a certain cannibalistic quality; for while it fosters a vested interest in promoting civil rights by some, it also creates a vested interest in *opposing* civil rights by the majority. Until this tendency is checked and overcome, we are in real danger of throwing out the baby with the bath water—abandoning our commitment to the ideal of civil rights in the process of rejecting demands for special outcomes and entitlements with which civil rights are mistakenly associated.

1

Origins of the Quest

The principles underlying the quest for civil rights trace their roots to the same fertile intellectual soil that produced the American Revolution. Martin Luther King reflected upon this development nearly two centuries later, observing that the civil rights vision "took from John Locke of England the theory of natural rights and the justification of revolution and imbued it with the ideal of a society governed by the people."[1]

This unique philosophical synthesis constituted an epochal development in the evolution of Western societies. The notion that individuals derived their rights from nature rather than at the sufferance of a sovereign emerged as the defining characteristic of the Revolutionary psyche, and distinguished the American experiment from its European forebears. Lord Acton remarked that

> Europe seemed incapable of becoming the home of free States. It was from America that the plain ideas that men ought to mind their own business, and that the nation is responsible to Heaven for the acts of the State—ideas long locked in the breasts of solitary thinkers, and hidden among Latin folios— burst forth like a conquerer upon the world they were destined to transform, under the title of the Rights of Man.[2]

These "rights of man" formed the foundation for the American concept of civil rights. Locke postulated that before society, men were born on earth in a state of perfect freedom. Nature bestowed upon all individuals certain basic rights that were essential to their survival—the right to life, liberty, and the fruits of their efforts.

Men were distinguished from lower creatures by virtue of their capacity to reason. This reason caused them to observe the one constraint that was necessary to preserve a state of maximum liberty—the rule that a man's rights are limited by the equal rights of others. This was the "law of nature" as defined by Locke—"no one ought to harm another in his life, liberty, or

5

possessions."[3] Only by observing this law could man expect that his own rights would be respected.

Locke recognized, however, that whereas rights are equal in nature, power is not. Consequently, he reasoned that individuals agree with their neighbors to form "social contracts," creating "societies" for the sole purpose of more effectively protecting their natural rights. Society is thus a volitional entity that derives its existence from the consent of its constituents. But the power of society is necessarily circumscribed by the law of nature—since no individual possesses the right to invade the rights of others, he cannot bestow upon society the right to do so. Consequently, a society acts in accordance with natural law only when it scrupulously observes the sanctity of individual rights.

Locke's conception of natural rights was adopted as the guiding philosophy of the American Revolution, and the social contract formed the blueprint for the proposed government. The principal revolutionary philosophers shared these basic tenets, which were forcefully propounded by Thomas Jefferson, Patrick Henry, Benjamin Franklin, George Mason, and others. But more than any of his compatriots, Thomas Paine understood the necessity of basing the moral justification of the new nation on the protection of "civil rights." In his writings during America's formative years, he established the definition of civil rights and the proper role of the state in preserving them, a definition that would endure for two hundred years.

Paine's definition of civil rights is based upon the concept of natural rights. He explained that civil rights are created by virtue of the social contract among individuals upon forming a society—a "civil right" is "a natural right exchanged."[4] Paine described this process in *The Rights of Man*:

> Man did not enter into society to become *worse* than he was before, nor to have less rights than he had before, but to have those rights better secured. His natural rights are the foundation of all of his civil rights. . . . Natural rights are those which always appertain to man in right of his existence. . . . Civil rights are those which appertain to man in right of his being a member of society. Every civil right has for its foundation some natural right pre-existing in the individual, but to which his individual power is not, in all cases, sufficiently competent.[5]

Paine thus maintained that a perfect identity exists between natural and civil rights; the only distinction is in the differing contexts of nature and society. He insisted that individuals surrender no part of their natural rights by exchanging them for civil rights; indeed, if this were not true there would be little incentive to form societies. Accordingly, society's authority is limited to protecting those rights. Paine argued that "the power produced by the aggregate of natural rights, imperfect in power in the individual, cannot be applied to invade the natural rights which are retained in the individual."[6] Every individual thus continues to enjoy maximum liberty, and society may not impose its collective mandate upon him—regardless of the breadth of the popular will.

This focus upon the individual is one of the most critical facets of the civil rights vision, and has provided the cornerstone for every major civil rights proclamation and enactment for nearly two hundred years. Its importance also explains its endurance. The individual is the least common denominator in society. Every individual is a member of some minority as well as some majority, and the distinction is necessarily amorphous and fleeting. If rights are subject to compromise by a particular combination among members of society at any given time, they will rapidly dissipate as the majority seeks to gain special privileges at the expense of the minority. Since the most vulnerable minority is the minority of one, rights can persist only if they are absolute and inhere in every individual. The architects of the American experiment understood that fundamental rights must be immune from majoritarian passions, and that the principal purpose of government is to preserve individual rights.[7]

No less critical to the vitality and endurability of the civil rights vision is the principle of the absolute equality of rights. In a state of nature, individuals make all decisions for themselves, while in a larger society, those matters that do not affect fundamental rights are amenable to democratic decision-making. But Paine and others recognized that an unchecked democratic system posed grave dangers to individual rights. A system in which rights could be compromised through the coercive power of the legislature was antithetical to the social contract. Paine explained that

> [i]n a state of nature, all men are equal in rights but they are not equal in power; the weak cannot protect themselves against the strong. This being the case, the institution of civil society is for the purpose of making an equalization of powers that shall be parallel to, and a guarantee of, the equality of rights. The laws of a country, when properly constructed, apply to this purpose.[8]

Paine underscored the importance of this principle by stressing that "[w]henever I use the words *freedom* or *rights*, I desire to mean a perfect equality of them. . . . It is this broad base, this universal foundation, that gives security to all and every part of society."[9]

In addition to its philosophical underpinnings, the principle of equality of rights has enormous practical value, the ramifications of which were not lost upon the revolutionary philosophers. "In a political view of the case," observed Paine, "the strength and permanent security of government is in proportion to the number of people interested in supporting it. The true policy therefore is to interest the whole by an equality of rights."[10]

Similarly, by vesting rights equally in all individuals, the whole of society's constituents is interested in resisting invasions of substantive rights by the state, thus providing a vital check against tyranny. The principle of equality of rights, Paine declared, is "clear and simple," for "where the rights of man are equal, every man must finally see the necessity of protecting the rights of others as the most effectual security for his own."[11] A member of a majority who clamors to subordinate rights asserted by a minority thereby establishes the precedent by which his own rights may be compromised in the future. There is simply no principled basis upon which to define exceptions to the rule. Paine displayed remarkable prescience in warning that whenever we

> depart from the principle of equal rights, or attempt any modification of it, we plunge into a labyrinth of difficulties from which there is no way out but by retreating. Where are we to stop? Or by what principle are we to find out the point to stop at, that shall discriminate between men of the same country, part of whom shall be free, and the rest not?[12]

The absolute equality of rights, then, creates a universally shared vested interest in the inviolability of individual rights—a particularly distinctive phenomenon noted by Alexis de Tocqueville during his American odyssey in the 1840s. "In America," he observed, "the lowest classes have conceived a very high notion of political rights, because they exercise those rights; and they refrain from attacking the rights of others in order that their own may not be violated."[13]

But the principle of equal rights does not operate solely to maintain civil order; it also restrains the rich and powerful from exploiting their position to invade the rights of the less powerful. Paine observed that "the rich have no more right to exclude the poor from the right of voting, or of electing and being elected, than the poor have a right to exclude the rich."[14] He warned that "[t]his opinion has already been fatal to thousands, who, not contented with *equal rights,* have sought more till they lost all, and experienced in themselves the degrading *inequality* they endeavored to fix upon others."[15]

While the universal interest in equal protection of rights provides the primary check against abuses, the ultimate check, however, is the right of rebellion. Any departure from the principle of equal rights "implies a stigma on the moral character of the persons excluded," proclaimed Paine, "and this is what no part of the community has a right to pronounce upon another part."[16] Moreover, continued Paine, any deprivation or exclusion "is a question of force, and not of right."[17] Whenever the principle of equality is violated, the violators forfeit their own right to equal protection of the laws; in essence, the law of reason is displaced by the rule of force. With the experience of the American Revolution fresh in his mind, Paine warned that it is possible to exclude individuals from their rights, "but it is impossible to exclude them from the right of rebelling against that exclusion; and when all other rights are taken away the right of rebellion is made perfect."[18] As subsequent history has repeatedly demonstrated, Paine's prediction of the dire consequences inevitably flowing from any methodical deprivation of equal rights is not exaggerated.

This emphasis on equality by Paine and his compatriots is not without its pitfalls, however, since the term is susceptible to varying definitions with widely divergent ramifications. Does "equality" translate into equal opportunity or equality in result? This distinction is seminal because the two definitions are fundamentally at odds with one another. On this issue, the architects of the civil rights vision were unequivocal—they clearly defined equality in terms of equal opportunity. In maintaining fidelity with the natural rights philosophy, no other choice was possible. The essence of the social contract is that it incorporates into society the maximum individual liberty that existed in the state of nature. Equality in result, conversely, requires coercion by the state, which necessarily infringes upon the very individual rights for whose protection societies are formed. The definition of equality held by the revolutionary philosophers was subsequently expressed in the French Declaration of the Rights of Man in 1789: the law is "the same for all"; and "all being equal in its sight, are equally eligible to all honours, places and employments, according to their different abilities, without any other distinction than that of their virtues and talents."[19]

Paine recognized equality of opportunity would inevitably lead to some degree of inequality in material outcome. "That property will ever be unequal is certain," he remarked. "Industry, superiority of talents, dexterity of management, extreme frugality, fortunate opportunities, or the opposite, or the means of those things, will ever produce that effect."[20] The virtue of the concept of equal rights, however, is that it eliminates such arbitrary factors as class, race, and religion as determinants of material outcome. This principle, concludes F. A. Hayek, renders "inoffensive the inequalities that liberty necessarily produces."[21] He continues,

> From the fact that people are very different it follows that, if we treat them equally, the result must be inequality in their actual position, and that the only way to place them in an equal position would be to treat them differently. Equality before the law and material equality are therefore not only

different but are in conflict with each other; and we can achieve either the one or the other, but not both at the same time.[22]

Thus faced with two possible but antithetical definitions of equality, Hayek explains, the framers' choice was preordained—"the desire of making people more alike in their condition cannot be accepted as a justification for . . . discriminatory coercion."[23] Since coercion is inconsistent with individual rights, forced equality in result is fundamentally incompatible with the principles of civil rights.

The civil rights vision was thus premised upon three essential principles: fundamental rights, individualism, and equality under the law. These core principles provided both the philosophical foundation and moral justification for the revolution against the Crown. As de Tocqueville would later reflect, "[i]t was the idea of right that enabled men to define anarchy and tyranny."[24] James Otis typified the revolutionary philosophy when he invoked the principles of civil rights to call into question the legitimacy of the British government, declaring that "[t]he natural liberty of man is to be free from any superior power on earth, and not to be under the will or legislative authority of man, but only to have the law of nature for his rule."[25] He further charged that Parliament's laws, enforced against the colonists, "shall and ought to be equally binding, as upon the subjects of Great Britain within the realm."[26] Because the Crown failed to remedy these fundamental violations of civil rights, the right of revolution was perfected.

The highest expression of the principles of civil rights was provided by the Declaration of Independence, which through the influence of Thomas Jefferson paralleled the philosophy articulated by Locke, Paine, and their ideological brethren. The Declaration set forth the "self-evident" principles that "all men are created equal" and "endowed by their Creator with certain unalienable Rights," among which are "Life, Liberty and the pursuit of Happiness." In order "to secure these rights, Governments are instituted among Men, deriving their just powers from the consent of the governed." The Declaration at once justified a revolution to vindicate the wholesale violation of civil rights by the monarchy as it defined man's civil rights and established the philosophical charter for the new government.

The Declaration of Independence irrevocably committed America to the quest for civil rights. The Declaration's central significance was underscored nearly two centuries later in perhaps the most important speech in the history of the civil rights movement, as Martin Luther King, speaking at the Lincoln Memorial, solemnly proclaimed:

[W]e have come to our nation's Capital to cash a check. When the architects of our republic wrote the magnificent words of the Constitution and the Declaration of Independence, they were signing a promissory note to which every American was to fall heir. This note was a promise that all men would be guaranteed the unalienable rights of life, liberty, and the pursuit of happiness.[27]

The quest to fulfill this great promise has furnished the moral framework for the civil rights movement ever since it was formally launched by the Declaration of Independence in 1776. The principles enunciated by Paine and his compatriots are the "first principles" of civil rights, and our progress can only be measured in terms of our fidelity to them.

Notes

1. Martin Luther King, Jr., *Where Do We Go From Here: Chaos or Community?* (New York: Harper & Row, Publishers, 1967), p. 70.
2. Quoted in F.A. Hayek, *The Constitution of Liberty* (Chicago: The University of Chicago Press, 1960), p. 176.
3. John Locke, *Second Treatise of Government* (Indianapolis, In.: Hackett Publishing Co., 1980), p. 9.
4. Thomas Paine, *The Rights of Man*, in Harry Hayden Clark, ed., *Thomas Paine* (New York: Hill and Wang, 1961), p. 89.
5. Id., p. 88.
6. Id., p. 89.
7. The author is particularly indebted to Chairman Clarence Thomas of the Equal Employment Opportunity Commission for his insights into the seminal importance of individual rights.
8. Thomas Paine, *Dissertation on the First Principles of Government*, in Robert B. Dishman, ed., *Burke and Paine on Revolution and the Rights of Man* (New York: Charles Scribner's Sons, 1971), p. 200.
9. Thomas Paine, "A Serious Address to the People of Pennsylvania," in Dishman, id., p. 198 n.2.
10. Paine, *Dissertation*, p. 198.
11. Id., p. 201.
12. Id., p. 200.
13. Alexis de Tocqueville, *Democracy in America* (New York: Vintage Books, 1945), vol. I, p. 254.
14. Paine, *Dissertation*, p. 196.
15. Paine, *Dissertation*, p. 197 (emphasis supplied).
16. Id., p. 198.
17. Id., p. 196.
18. Id., p. 198.
19. *Declaration of the Rights of Man and of the Citizen*, art. 4, in Ian Browne, ed., *Basic Documents on Human Rights* (Oxford: Clarendon Press, 1971), p. 8.
20. Paine, *Dissertation*, p. 199.
21. Hayek, p. 85.
22. Id. at 87.
23. Id.

24. de Tocqueville, p. 254.
25. James Otis, "The Rights of the British Colonies asserted and proved," in Samuel Eliot Morison, ed., *Sources & Documents illustrating the American Revolution 1764-1788 and the formation of the Federal Constitution*, 2d ed. (London: Oxford University Press, 1970), p. 5.
26. Id.
27. Martin Luther King, Jr., "I Have a Dream," in Leon Friedman, ed., *The Civil Rights Reader* (New York: Walker and Company, 1967), p. 110-111.

2

Abolitionism: The Quest for Freedom

Having embraced the most liberating moral philosophy in the history of mankind, the revolutionary philosophers were immediately impelled to confront the very antithesis of their philosophy—the institution of human slavery.

Ironically, slavery (though not the slave trade) was already repudiated in Great Britain, revolution against which had been justified as a matter of civil rights. Indeed, Sir William Blackstone had observed just prior to the American Revolution in his classic *Commentaries on the Law of England* that slavery is utterly inconsistent with any conception of civil rights, and he rejected the rationales advanced to support it. Blackstone averred that slavery is not justifiable on the basis of war, since "[w]ar itself is justifiable only on principles of self-preservation, and therefore it gives no other right over prisoners but merely to disable them from doing harm to us," and then only for the duration of the war.[1] Similarly, slavery cannot be premised on tacit consent, since every contract requires a *quid pro quo*, and "what equivalent can be given for life and liberty, both of which, in absolute slavery, are held to be in the master's disposal?"[2] Thus, slavery was antithetical to freedom of contract, the cornerstone of a free society.

Slavery was a stark anomaly in the midst of the American conception of civil rights, embodied within what Gunnar Myrdal later called the "American Creed"—the "ideals of the essential dignity of the individual human being, of the fundamental equality of all men, and of certain inalienable rights to freedom, justice, and a fair opportunity."[3] Yet, at the very moment of great triumph for human liberty, America tragically chose to sanction the most profound and demeaning nullification of that liberty. The nation thus assumed from the outset what Martin Luther King referred to as a "schizophrenic personality,"[4] which would afflict it and plague the quest for civil rights for nearly two hundred years.

Slavery was established in America long before the civil rights vision that would eventually confront it. The first Negro slaves were imported into the

Jamestown colony in 1619.[5] An antislavery response emerged as early as 1688, with the declaration by Pennsylvania Quakers that "[h]ere is liberty of conscience, which is right and reasonable; here ought to be likewise liberty of body."[6]

The early antislavery movement was religiously inspired, but religious tenets were soon subsumed by the political principles of the revolutionary era as the primary focus of abolitionism. Period historian Winthrop Jordan recounts that opponents of slavery quickly came to argue that "[a]ll men, including Negroes, shared in 'natural' rights because they were men, not because they were candidates for immortality."[7] They charged that "Negro slavery loomed as a flagrant violation of the new ideal of a society composed of equal and therefore free individuals and in which there was equality of contractual power among the constituent members of society."[8] Indeed, slavery was incompatible not only with America's political revolution, but with its burgeoning capitalist economic revolution as well. George Mason complained that slavery discouraged arts and manufactures;[9] while Adam Smith assailed the inherent inefficiency of slavery, which rendered it "altogether inconvenient."[10]

Taken at face value, the revolutionary principles would necessarily spell doom for the institution of slavery. As Gunnar Myrdal observed, slaves "could not possibly have invented a system of ideals which better corresponded to their interests."[11] Understandably, many slaves viewed these principles as cause for optimism, as reflected in a petition for freedom during the Revolution by a group of slaves, who declared that "[e]very principle from which America has acted in the course of her difficulties with Great-Britain, pleads stronger than a thousand arguments for your Petitioners."[12]

The manifest inconsistency of slavery with the principles of civil rights was starkly apparent to the revolutionary philosophers. Many of them spoke out against slavery, among them Paine, Jefferson, John Adams, Benjamin Franklin, Alexander Hamilton, Patrick Henry, John Jay, James Madison, James Monroe, and George Washington.[13] Yet, many of these same men were themselves slaveholders, underscoring the inconsistency with which they confronted this critical issue. At least one of their contemporaries, Dr. Benjamin Rush, decried this hypocrisy: "It would be useless for us to denounce the servitude to which the Parliament of Great Britain wishes to reduce us, while we continue to keep our fellow creatures in slavery just because their color is different from ours."[14]

Some attempts were made to reconcile practice with principles. Jefferson, supported by Adams and Franklin, urged the Continental Congress to apply the revolutionary principles to condemn slavery. His original draft of the Declaration of Independence contained an explicit provision denouncing King George for

> wag[ing] cruel war against human nature itself, violating its most sacred rights of life and liberty in the persons of a distant people who never offended him. . . . Determined to keep open a market where MEN should be bought and sold, he has prostituted his negative for suppressing every legislative attempt to prohibit or to restrain this execrable commerce.[15]

But a powerful economic incentive to perpetuate slavery was growing in the American South, in the form of cotton. While the North was becoming increasingly industrialized, the Southern economy was based in large part upon feudal-style plantations, with slaves as the modern-day serfs. Accordingly, the Southern delegation successfully pressured Congress to delete Jefferson's condemnation of the slave trade—a profound capitulation whose ramifications continue to haunt the American conscience even today.

Yet even without Jefferson's explicit antislavery provision, the principles embodied in the Declaration of Independence—whose language makes no exceptions based upon skin color or social status, and which in fact implicitly forbids such exceptions by embracing the ideal of equality— clearly conflict with the legitimacy of involuntary servitude. In order to justify the existence of slavery in a society committed to freedom, then, the pro-slavery advocates would have to repudiate the principles underlying the new republic and concoct some philosophical justification for their coercive practices.

Such a rationale would provide the original justification for drawing distinctions in rights on the basis of race in America. It was accomplished through a tortured interpretation of the "social contract," focusing upon the acquisition of civil rights by individuals as they "enter" society. Locke and Paine, of course, believed that the rights that individuals acquire upon entering society are nothing more than the natural rights that preexist in the state of nature; men "exchange" natural rights for civil rights when they form or join societies. British jurisprudence, however, literally interpreted the notion of acquiring civil rights upon "entering" society , i.e., civil rights accrue to individuals only when they *physically* enter society; thus, slaves lacked civil rights until they actually set foot on British soil, whereupon they acquired such rights.[16]

The pro-slavery theorists took this approach a step further, viewing entrance into society not in terms of physical presence but of moral "fitness"—slaves were something less than men, they contended, and consequently they were unfit to enter society and to assume the civil rights to which they would then be entitled. To attain any semblance of logical consistency, this construction required—and in part gave rise to—the mythology of the inferiority of blacks. If blacks were innately inferior, they could never hope to join society on an equal footing. Accepting this premise, slavery was thus not only morally justified, but absolutely necessary since slaves were incapable of rationally conducting their own affairs; in the natural order of things, blacks would always have to rely upon their white masters for their well-being. The concept of *noblesse oblige*—that everyone would be satisfied if proper roles in society were maintained—provided a beneficent, paternalistic facade for the ideology of slavery.[17]

Thus were the parameters for debate over the issue of slavery defined as the framers approached the task of forging national unity and crafting a Constitution in the decade following the Revolution. Patrick Henry personified the agonizing conflict between principles and political realities facing the new republic, exclaiming that "it would rejoice my very soul that every one of my fellow-beings was emancipated. . . . But is it practicable, by any human means, to liberate them without producing the most dreadful and ruinous consequences?"[18]

To their credit, the framers crafted a magnificent and enduring document creating a government of limited powers. The influence of the natural rights philosophy was apparent throughout the document, and was directly incorporated through the Ninth Amendment, which established that "[t]he enumeration in the Constitution, of certain rights, shall not be construed to deny or disparage others retained by the people"; and the Tenth Amendment, which reserved to the states and the people all powers not specifically delegated to the federal government.

But on the matter of slavery, the framers were unable or unwilling to apply these general principles. Instead of laying the slavery issue to rest once and for all, the framers succumbed to intense sectional pressures and compromised on the issue, ignoring the objections of Paine and others that any compromise on such a seminal issue would amount to a negation of civil rights.

The first part of this infamous compromise merely postponed the issue—Article I, section 9 of the Constitution provided that Congress could not prohibit the slave trade until 1808. The implications of the second facet of the compromise were even more troubling, for in the name of political expediency it sanctioned the notion that blacks were less than men. In debating how to count population for the purpose of apportioning congressional representation among the states, the Northern delegates expediently argued that slaves should not be included, for this would inflate Southern population and hence its congressional representation; while the

South, most ironically, argued that slaves should be counted. The resulting compromise, embodied in Article I, section 2 of the Constitution, counted slaves as three-fifths of men. This affirmation of inequality, thus established in the fundamental law of the land, would undercut the credibility of subsequent arguments to the contrary by Northern abolitionists and legitimize the contention that blacks were inferior and incapable of entering society or exercising civil rights.

Building upon this premise, Southern pro-slavery theorists repudiated their remaining antislavery statesmen, who as late as 1775 had denounced slavery as an "unnatural practice" whose abolition was "the greatest object of desire."[19] Instead, the new Southern intelligentsia methodically crafted an ideology of slavery as a "positive good."[20] These theorists sowed the seeds for the South's sordid record on civil rights by resuscitating the ancient Greek philosophy that man has no rights save those bestowed upon him by the state, and that such rights should be apportioned on the basis of status. Since slaves occupied the lowest possible status, they were entitled to no rights.[21] But pursuant to the practice of *noblesse oblige*, whites would provide for the needs of blacks. This ideology was perfectly suited to the burgeoning Southern feudal aristocracy, and was promoted as a bulwark against the evils of capitalism.[22]

By failing to eradicate slavery, the framers left unhealed a mortal wound that would continue to fester and gnaw at the national conscience. This abdication of principle over the issue of slavery presented the quest for civil rights with its first "crisis of victory" in the aftermath of the revolutionary triumph. These crises, endemic to the civil rights movement, are in part an unfortunate byproduct of its underlying philosophy. Civil rights advocates have traditionally required a breathing period after great triumphs—a time of reflection, introspection, and debate—to define the most serious remaining impediments and to craft the most effective courses of action. The civil rights vision does not automatically suggest any definite "program"— the appropriate strategy at any point in time depends upon the particular deprivations of civil rights that may exist; and as the obstacles change and grow more subtle, the task of confronting them in a manner consistent with the principles of civil rights becomes more difficult. As F. A. Hayek explains, the civil rights philosophy is often characterized as "merely negative":

> This is true in the sense that peace is also a negative concept or that security or quiet or the absence of any particular impediment or evil is negative. It is to this class of concepts that liberty belongs: it describes the absence of a particular obstacle—coercion by other men. It becomes positive only through what we make of it.[23]

Thus, whether a crisis of victory would lead to triumph or tragedy would depend upon whether the advocates of civil rights could translate their principles into a positive agenda to respond to the important civil rights issues of the day.

Those who remained faithful to the principles of civil rights following the Revolution were caught within such a crisis of victory. The Revolution had scored an enormous triumph for civil rights by establishing the fundamental principles of individual sovereignty and equality of rights. But the pro-slavery ideology was growing in virulence as well as in its number of adherents. Confronted with this challenge, the advocates of civil rights recognized that simply to declare that certain rights existed was insufficient—they must produce a practical program to combat slavery, or witness their precious principles reduced to a practical nullity. Some of the revolutionary protagonists applied their principles to the cause of abolition—Paine, for instance, authored a "high-toned preamble" to Pennsylvania's emancipation act[24]; Franklin, Hamilton, and Jay organized abolition societies.[25] But it was left to a new generation of leaders to effectively confront the issues of the Nineteenth Century.

From the crisis of victory following the Revolution emerged the abolition movement. The goal of the movement was to abolish slavery and to establish the principles of civil rights as part of the fundamental law of the land. Historian James M. McPherson recounts that the "antislavery crusade . . . envisaged not only a negative freedom—the absence of chattelism—but a positive guaranty of equal protection of the law to all men."[26]

For the first half century following ratification of the Constitution, the abolition movement was moderate and pursued essentially incremental advances. The early movement utilized two primary techniques to achieve its aims—manumission and education. The first tactic involved raising money to purchase slaves for the purpose of turning them free. But this strategy, while effective in liberating a significant number of slaves, was viewed as undesirable by many abolitionists because it implicitly sanctioned the notion that slaves were "property" for which their owners were entitled to compensation.[27]

The second strategy, education, built upon the first. In the South, education for slaves was generally unlawful,[28] rendering the myth of black inferiority a self-fulfilling prophecy. But in the North, abolitionists were dedicated to providing educational opportunities to the "free persons of color," who by the time of the Civil War accounted for 11% of all blacks in America, in large part due to manumission efforts. While limited to this small segment of the black population, these educational efforts were nonetheless vitally important because they produced a core of educated blacks who assumed leadership roles following the Civil War.[29]

Most early educational opportunities for blacks were provided by the private sector, in institutions such as the African Free School in New York, which became a public school in 1834 after 47 years of private operation.[30] Other schools providing access to free blacks were established by abolitionists, particularly the Tappan family. Lewis Tappan, for instance, directed the highly successful interracial Oneida Institute in New York, supported the Lane Theological Seminary in Ohio, and refounded Oberlin College.[31]

Meanwhile, almost all public schools were segregated, reflecting the wide acceptance of the myth of black inferiority and frustrating attempts to secure meaningful educational opportunities for free blacks. In 1849, the Tappans hired Charles Sumner to challenge school segregation under the equal protection clause of the Massachusetts Constitution.[32] Sumner invoked the core principle of equal rights in his argument to the Massachusetts Supreme Court, an argument that set the standard for civil rights advocacy:

> The equality which was declared by our fathers in 1776 . . . was equality before the law. Its object was to efface all political or civil distinctions. . . . This is the Great Charter of every person who draws his breath upon this soil. . . .[H]e is a MAN, the equal of all his fellow-men.[33]

Although the court rejected Sumner's argument, the abolitionists continued their efforts and finally convinced the Massachusetts legislature to open public schools on an equal basis in 1855.[34]

Despite the notable successes of manumission and education, a sense of frustration permeated the movement by the 1830s, as it became clear that it was far from achieving its ultimate goals. This frustration was personified by Nat Turner, a religious fanatic, who led an ill-fated uprising in 1831 that killed some sixty whites—along with whatever anti-slavery sentiment remained in the South.[35]

The Turner rebellion was seized upon to confirm the Southern perception of blacks as something less than men, and it fanned the flames of reaction. President Andrew Jackson, for instance, sought legislation in 1835 to counteract "the painful excitement produced in the South by attempts to circulate through the mails inflammatory appeals addressed to the passions of the slaves," by banning the delivery of "incendiary publications intended to instigate" them.[36] Congressman John Quincy Adams responded that Jackson's request made it clear that the slave power was becoming "the disgrace and degradation of my country, trampling in the dust the first principle of human liberty."[37] Although the legislation was defeated, many postmasters nonetheless intercepted the mail in question on their own initiative.[38]

Abolitionists drew important lessons from the episode. Francis Jackson observed in 1835 that the "gag laws" devised by the proponents of slavery

> betray the essential rottenness of the cause . . . they are meant to strengthen. . . . Happily, one point seems already to be gaining universal assent, that slavery cannot long survive free discussion. Hence the efforts of the friends and apologists to break down this right. And hence the immense stake, which the enemies of slavery hold, in its preservation. The contest is therefore substantially between liberty and slavery.[39]

Thus did the abolitionists come to more fully appreciate their vested interest in civil rights—the necessity of protecting the rights of others as the only effectual security for their own.

The abolitionists responded to these challenges by intensifying their efforts. The new, more radical approach was launched by William Lloyd Garrison, who, along with James G. Birney, Theodore Weld, Lewis Tappan, and freeman Frederick Douglass, formed the philosophical vanguard of the movement. Garrison eloquently conveyed the sense of urgency for the great push forward and commitment to moral absolutes in his first issue of *The Liberator* in 1831:

> I will be harsh as truth, and as uncompromising as justice. On this subject, I do not wish to think, or speak, or write, with moderation. No! No! Tell a man whose house is on fire to give a moderate alarm; tell him to moderately rescue his wife from the hands of the ravisher; . . . but urge me not to use moderation in a cause like the present. I am in earnest—I will not equivocate—I will not excuse—I will not retreat a single inch—AND I WILL BE HEARD.[40]

Garrison interpreted the principles of civil rights literally and absolutely. He lambasted the clergy for its ambivalence on the slavery issue, demanded equal rights for women, and refused to exercise the franchise in a government that included slaveholders.[41] In 1833, he and the other leading abolitionists founded the American Anti-Slavery Society, through which much of their efforts would henceforth be channeled.[42] In its "Declaration of Sentiments," the Society declared that its activities were necessary to effectuate the intent of the Declaration of Independence. The Society rejected the practice of manumission because compensation for slaveholders offended the "fundamental principle that man cannot hold property in man." Instead, the Society demanded that blacks "be admitted forthwith to the enjoyment of the same privileges, and the exercise of the same prerogatives, as others."[43]

In the beginning, the Society's primary weapon was moral suasion, exercised through such organs as *The Liberator*. The mission was not an easy one. The struggle was typified by James Birney, a reformed slaveholder, who was driven out of Kentucky in 1835 by angry mobs incensed over his anti-slavery writings.[44] For Birney, the quest for abolition was far more than an end in itself:

> The contest is becoming—has become—one, not alone of freedom for the *black*, but of freedom for the *white*. It has become absolutely necessary, that slavery should cease in order that freedom may be preserved to any portion of our land. The antagonist principles of liberty and slavery have been roused and one or the other must be victorious. There will be no cessation of the strife until Slavery shall be exterminated or liberty destroyed.[45]

The stakes were high, and the battle lines drawn.

In 1839, the abolitionists added political action to their arsenal. Dissatisfied with the inclusion of slaveholders among both Democrats and Whigs, they formed the Liberty Party.[46] The party's platform was predicated upon a single issue—moral opposition to slavery and to the inequality of rights. The party believed, as did Garrison, that the Constitution in its existing form sanctioned slavery, and that abolition required a change in the Constitution.[47] Although the party fielded candidates and received strong support from blacks including Frederick Douglass, it enjoyed little success due to its narrow base and the severe limits upon black voting rights.[48]

Most abolitionists turned instead in 1848 to the Free Soil Party, which enjoyed somewhat broader appeal through its advocacy of "free soil, free speech, free labor, and free men."[49] The Free Soilers rejected the Liberty Party view that the Constitution sanctioned slavery, reasoning that the Constitution cannot "secure *general liberty* . . . and at the same time guaranty *local slavery*." Thus, all that was necessary for abolition was to enforce the Constitution.[50] The Free Soilers recruited former President Martin Van Buren as their presidential candidate, despite some qualms about his previous expressions of anti-abolition sentiments.[51] The election was won by Zachary Taylor, a Whig.

While the abolitionists were engaged in moral and political campaigns against slavery, the momentum was building toward the inevitable conflict of which Paine and Birney, among others, had warned. The first of a crucial series of provocations was the Fugitive Slave Law, one of five measures known collectively as the Compromise of 1850. The law obliterated any semblance of equal rights for purported runaway slaves, denying them the right to testify and to receive a jury trial, while presuming their guilt.[52] By formally reducing blacks to property rather than human status, the law engendered enormous public sympathy for the abolition cause.[53]

This enactment was followed seven years later by the infamous *Dred Scott* decision, in which the Supreme Court finally confronted the issue of the Constitution's posture with respect to blacks. Dred Scott, an emancipated black, asserted jurisdiction to sue in the courts; but the Court held that as a non-citizen, he had no right to sue. Chief Justice Roger Taney framed the question as whether "a negro [can] become a member of the political community formed and brought into existence by the Constitution . . . and as such become entitled to all the rights . . . guaranteed by that instrument to the citizen."[54] Taney conceded that the words of the Declaration of Independence "would seem to embrace the whole human family," but charged that if the framers, many of whom owned slaves, had purported to extend equal rights to blacks, "the conduct of the[se] distinguished men . . . would have been utterly and flagrantly inconsistent with the principles they asserted."[55] In resolving the question of whether the framers of the Constitution intended to give any rights to emancipated blacks, the Court concluded they had not:

> On the contrary, [blacks] were at that time considered as a subordinate and inferior class of beings, who had been subjugated by the dominant race, and whether emancipated or not, yet remained subject to their authority, and had no rights or privileges but such as those who held the power and the government might choose to grant them.[56]

The *Dred Scott* ruling thus utterly repudiated the principles of civil rights, and elevated into constitutional law the perverted ideology of the pro-slavery advocates. Combined with the Fugitive Slave Law, the *Dred Scott* decision strongly suggested that the subordination of civil rights was complete, and that the only recourse was rebellion.

Among those drawing this conclusion was abolitionist John Brown and eighteen followers, who responded by raiding a government arsenal at Harper's Ferry in Autumn, 1859. The purpose of the raid, according to John Copeland, one of five blacks involved, was to gain "freedom to at least a few of my poor and enslaved brethren who have been most foully and unjustly deprived of their liberty."[57] Tactically, the raid was ill-conceived—ten were killed, and Brown was quickly tried and hanged, but he became a martyr to the abolition cause.[58]

The *Dred Scott* decision also convinced the Free Soilers that their approach—enforcement of what they perceived as constitutional guarantees of equal rights—was inadequate. Consequently, they joined with anti-slavery Whigs and Democrats to form the Republican Party.[59] The abolition movement was finally a part of political organization capable of winning a national election and implementing the abolitionist agenda.

As the Republican presidential nominee in 1860, Abraham Lincoln was thrust to the forefront of the debate over slavery. Although Lincoln opined that blacks were physiologically inferior to whites, he believed in the *moral* equality of all men—the Jeffersonian view that all humans possess in equal measure a moral faculty that sets them apart from animals and renders them capable of self-accountability.[60] Lincoln further believed that equality was the defining characteristic of republican government, and that "[t]he entire records of the world . . . may be searched in vain for one single affirmation . . . that the negro was not included in the Declaration of Independence.[61] Slavery, he lamented, "forces so many really good people amongst ourselves into an open war with the very fundamental principles of civil liberty."[62]

The Democrats split into two factions supporting different candidates in the 1860 election—John Breckenridge, representing the South, and Stephen Douglas from the North. Douglas shared the view expressed by Taney in *Dred Scott* that in a democracy, the majority may deny equal rights in the exercise of its right of self-government.[63] But Lincoln responded that when Douglas "invites any people willing to have slavery, to establish it, he is blowing out the moral lights around us."[64] Lincoln declared that

> [i]f the Negro *is* a man, is it not to that extent a total destruction of self-government, to say that he too shall not govern *himself*? When the white man governs himself that is self-government; but when he governs himself and also governs *another* man, that is more than self-government; this is despotism.[65]

Lincoln thus exposed the tenuous ideological underpinnings of slavery, and with his election, the South felt impelled to withdraw from the Union. Alexander Stephens, the vice president of the Confederacy, revealed how far the Southern ideology had strayed from the principles of civil rights:

> The prevailing ideas entertained by . . . most of the leading statesmen at the time of the formation of the old Constitution, were that the enslavement of the African was in violation of the laws of nature: that it was wrong in principle, socially, morally, and politically. . . . Those ideas were fundamentally wrong. They rested upon the assumption of the equality of the races. This was an error.[66]

Stephens went on to set forth the philosophical premises of the Southern rebellion:

> Our new government is founded upon exactly the opposite idea; its foundations are laid, its cornerstone rests upon the great truth that the Negro is not the equal of the white man. That slavery, the subordination to the superior race, is his natural and normal condition.[67]

With these words, the ideological battle lines were clearly established. The ensuing Civil War would determine which of the contradictory philosophical views would prevail.

For Lincoln, the primary goal of the war was to preserve the republic; but for the abolitionists, the objective was to re-establish the principles of civil rights, thus ensuring a society, as described by Wendell Phillips, in which there is "no native, no foreigner, no black, no white, no German, no Saxon; . . . only American citizens, with one impartial law over all."[68] The abolitionists thus provided the moral high ground for those, like Lincoln, whose goals were pragmatic rather than philosophical.

In the end, the war accomplished both ends. Slavery was formally abolished in 1865 with the passage of the Thirteenth Amendment. But the abolition movement's business was unfinished—it still faced the task of ensuring that the principles vindicated by the war would endure as a permanent feature of the American system.

The initial problem facing the abolitionists and their congressional allies, the "radical" Republicans, was the mass social dislocation following abolition and the defeat of the South. In response, troops were dispatched to restore order, and Congress passed the Freedmen Acts, providing aid and allocating confiscated land to former slaves and loyal refuges. The acts established the practice of providing restitution to actual victims of civil rights deprivations at the expense of those responsible for them.[69]

Once some stability was assured, the abolitionists turned their attention to finishing their mission. They recognized that their principles could survive future assaults only if permanently engrafted upon the fundamental law of the land. Their chosen vehicle was a constitutional guarantee of equal protection of the laws, which would forever render irrelevant distinctions in rights based upon race or color. As Frederick Douglass wrote to President Andrew Johnson, "Peace between races is not to be secured by degrading one race and exalting another, but by maintaining a state of equal justice between all classes."[70] This equality would provide an opportunity for blacks to strive forward unimpeded by artificial restraints or paternalism. Wendell Phillips proclaimed, "Let us . . . claim for the Negro JUSTICE, not privileges; RIGHTS, not alms."[71]

The South reacted immediately and in predictable fashion. Deprived of the assistance of the Fugitive Slave Laws and limited by the presence of troops in their ability to enforce their will by physical force, former slaveholders turned to their state legislatures to restore as closely as practicable the feudal social order that prevailed before the war. George Fitzhugh, a leading pro-slavery advocate, urged, "We must have a black code." Fitzhugh reasoned,

Nature never intended, and never will permit the races to live together, except as masters and slaves, so that the superior race, commanding the labor of the inferior race, shall at the same time be compelled to provide for, and take care of that race. We do not mean by slavery such as that which has been recently abolished, but some sort of subordination of the inferior race that will compel them to labor, whilst it protects their rights and provides for their wants.[72]

Couched in these benevolent terms, Fitzhugh's argument was surely the earliest form of what has come in recent years to be known as "benign discrimination"—the implicit assumptions of which reveal it, like all forms of racism, to be anything but benign.

Eight Southern states heeded Fitzhugh's admonition, enacting Black Codes between 1865-67. These codes, which would subsequently re-appear in an even more virulent, all-encompassing form known as Jim Crow laws, were primarily aimed at restricting labor market opportunities through vagrancy and apprenticeship laws.[73] The South Carolina Black Code, for instance, enacted in 1865, subjected virtually all conditions of labor and entrepreneurship to pervasive state control. Under the code, a "servant" could lawfully leave his master's employ only for an insufficient supply of wholesome food, an unauthorized battery against the servant or his family, an invasion of his conjugal rights, or failure to pay wages when due. Moreover, "person[s] of color" were required to procure a license from the local court in order to "practice the . . . business of an artisan, mechanic, or shop-keeper, or any other trade, employment or business." Such a license, valid only for one year, required a showing of skill, fitness, and good moral character; plus an annual payment of the sum—certainly staggering to the property-less emancipated slaves—of $100. Furthermore, the license required an apprenticeship or existing practice, and could be revoked upon any complaint of abuse.[74] These restrictions—forerunners to the similarly stifling licensing laws that limit entrepreneurial opportunities for minorities today—weaved a tangled web of pitfalls and disincentives that utterly precluded meaningful participation in the economy for the newly emancipated blacks.

And as if these impediments were inadequate, the tacticians for this racist agenda added yet additional burdens in the form of vagrancy laws. These laws rendered freedom of movement all but impossible by subjecting anyone without a fixed abode and lawful and reputable employment—however temporary the condition—to a year's imprisonment and/or hard labor.[75] Under the guise of paternalism, the subjugation of blacks, accomplished through the coercive power of the state, was once again complete.

These were precisely the types of wholesale civil rights deprivations that the abolitionists feared, and they moved swiftly to counteract them. The radical Republicans in Congress pushed through the Civil Rights Act of

1866. The act embraced the traditional concept of civil rights, defined by Rep. James F. Wilson, the bill's floor manager, as "the absolute rights of individuals, such as 'the right of personal security, the right of personal liberty, and the right to acquire and enjoy property.'"[76] Even more importantly, the act was designed to affirm the universality of civil rights—that "[i]n respect to all civil rights, ... there is to be hereafter no distinction between the white race and the black race."[77] The act clearly established, for the first time, that all persons born in the United States—regardless of color—are citizens; and that all citizens

> have the same right [to] make and enforce contracts, to sue, be parties, and give evidence, to inherit, purchase, lease, sell, hold, and convey real and personal property, and to full and equal benefit of all laws [for] the security of persons and property, as is enjoyed by white citizens, and shall be subject to like punishment, [and] to none other, any law ... to the contrary notwithstanding.[78]

President Johnson vetoed the act, questioning its constitutionality, but Congress overrode his veto.[79] Though fortified by this victory, the abolitionists had learned well the lessons of the past; heeding Johnson's warning of the act's constitutional vulnerability, they moved to imprint the rule of color-blindness in the Constitution itself. Although the Fifth Amendment already provided restraints against *federal* invasions of civil rights, the radical Republicans recognized that *state* governments were crafting the most serious deprivations, and they determined to establish once and for all that states cannot make distinctions among their citizens on the basis of race. The Fourteenth Amendment, ratified in 1868, accomplished this end, creating what would become the principal instrument in challenging state-sanctioned racial discrimination in the years ahead. The amendment constitutionalized the color-blind provisions of the Civil Rights Act, providing that

> [n]o State shall make or enforce any law which shall abridge the privileges or immunities of citizens of the United States; nor shall any State deprive any person of life, liberty, or property, without due process of law; nor deny to any person within its jurisdiction the equal protection of the laws.

The amendment thus embedded in the Constitution the fundamental principles of civil rights. As Senator David Clark proclaimed, "The negro is a man! and ... [is] entitled to be treated by us as a man, and to demand and enjoy the same political privileges as other men."[80] The essence of the amendment, declared Senator Thaddeus Stevens, was that henceforth "no distinction would be tolerated in this purified Republic but what arose from merit and conduct."[81] Thus, the protection extended to everyone, whites as well as blacks, leading Frederick Douglass to ridicule a colleague who suggested proportional representation for blacks in government appointments. Declaring that "equality of numbers has nothing to do with equality of attainments," Douglass chided,

> Upon your statistical principle, the colored people ought, therefore, not only to hold one-eighth of all the offices in the country, but they should own one-eighth of all the property, and pay one-eighth of all the taxes of the Country. Equal in numbers, they should, of course, be equal in everything else. They should constitute one-eighth of the poets, statesmen, scholars, authors, and philosophers of the country.[82]

The message was clear: having won equality after a century of struggle, the black leadership was not about to sacrifice principle for expediency.

The radical Republicans took still further steps to protect civil rights, most notably the Fifteenth Amendment in 1870, which afforded protection for federal voting rights. And a year later, Congress passed the Civil Rights Act of 1871, creating a private right to sue for deprivations effectuated "under color of state law" of any rights secured by the Constitution and federal laws. This act opened the courthouse doors to victims of state-sanctioned civil rights violations that had been closed by the *Dred Scott* decision.

With the goals of the abolition movement thus apparently accomplished, a new crisis of victory began to arise. The pressure for reform began to fade, and the movement's aging leadership suggested little in the way of a future agenda. Moreover, massive corruption within the Grant administration eroded the credibility of the radical Republicans, and they began to jettison Reconstruction after the Democrats captured the House of Representatives in 1874 for the first time in eighteen years.[83] The disputed presidential election of 1876 led to a compromise with the Democrats providing for the removal of troops and the end of Reconstruction the following year. The abolitionist era came to an end with the death of William Lloyd Garrison in 1879, who warned prophetically that the "fundamental" issue of equal rights was being overshadowed by the "incidental" issue of corruption, and that Southern governments were being re-established "by the shot-gun policy, by bloody usurpation."[84] Indeed, at the very moment of the greatest triumph for civil rights since the American Revolution, the machinery was being set in motion to stifle the gains accomplished through years of struggle and conflict, perseverance and principle.

Yet regardless of what was to follow, the abolitionists' legacy was a proud one, providing compelling testimony that uncompromising fealty to the

principles of civil rights can produce revolutionary change. The abolitionists utterly discredited the notion that some individuals exist to serve
others, and proved beyond question that the principles embodied in the
American system are fundamentally at odds with those that would draw
distinctions on the basis of color and race.[85] However bleak the quest for
civil rights would appear at times in years hence, its advocates could—and
did—find inspiration in the courage, integrity, and achievements of their
abolitionist predecessors.

Notes

1. Albert P. Blaustein and Robert L. Zangrando, eds., *Civil Rights and the American Negro* (New York: Trident Press, 1968), p. 34.
2. Id., p. 35.
3. Gunnar Myrdal, *An American Dilemma* (New York: Harper & Brothers Publishers, 1944), p. 4.
4. King, *Where Do We Go From Here*, p. 68.
5. Blaustein and Zangrando, p. 4.
6. Brief for Appellants, *Brown v. Board of Education*, 347 U.S. 483 (1954) (filed
   November 16, 1953), p. 202 n.5. The brief provides one of the most complete
   and insightful accounts of the history of civil rights in America.
7. Winthrop D. Jordan, *White Over Black* (Chapel Hill, N.C.: University of North
   Carolina Press, 1968), p. 294.
8. Id., p. 295.
9. Morison, p. 283.
10. Adam Smith, *An Inquiry Into the Nature and Course of the Wealth of Nations*
    (Indianapolis: Liberty Classics, 1981), p. 389.
11. Myrdal, p. 13.
12. Gerald Sorin, *Abolitionism: A New Perspective* (New York: Praeger Publishers,
    1972), p. 31 (emphasis omitted).
13. Id., p. 30.
14. Id., p. 21.
15. Blaustein and Zangrando, p. 43-44.
16. Id., p. 34.
17. Robert Higgs, *Competition and Coercion* (Cambridge, England: Cambridge
    University Press, 1977), p. 7.
18. Morison, p. 354.
19. Sorin, p. 122.
20. Higgs, p. 7.
21. Brief for Appellants, p. 203 n.8.
22. Sorin, p. 124.
23. Hayek, p. 19.
24. Jordan, p. 302.
25. Dwight L. Dumond, "The Abolition Indictment of Slavery," in Hugh Hawkins,
    ed., *The Abolitionists: Means, Ends, and Motivations*, 2d ed. (Lexington, Ma.:
    D.C. Heath and Co., 1972), p. 43.
26. James M. McPherson, *The Struggle for Equality* (Princeton, N.J.: Princeton
    University Press, 1964), p. 221.

27. Benjamin Quarles, *Black Abolitionists* (New York: Oxford University Press, 1969), p. 11.
28. Joseph W. Scott, *The Black Revolts* (Cambridge, Ma.: Schenkman Publishing Co., Inc., 1976), p. 92.
29. Thomas Sowell, *Race and Economics* (New York: David McKay Co., 1975), p. 35.
30. Quarles, p. 13.
31. Sorin, p. 67.
32. Id., p. 68.
33. Blaustein and Zangrando, p. 113 (emphasis omitted).
34. Id., p. 122.
35. Quarles, p. 17-18.
36. Sorin, p. 130-31.
37. Id., p. 133.
38. Id., p. 131.
39. Id., p. 132-33.
40. Arthur Zilversmit, "The Abolitionists," in James C. Curtis and Lewis L. Gould, eds., *The Black Experience in America* (Austin, Tx.: University of Texas Press, 1970), p. 61.
41. Quarles, p. 42-43.
42. Id., p. 14.
43. American Anti-Slavery Society, "Declaration of Sentiments," in Hawkins, p. 52-54.
44. Dumond, p. 31-32.
45. Id.
46. Quarles, p. 183.
47. Sorin, p. 88.
48. Quarles, p. 169 and 183-85.
49. Id., p. 185.
50. Sorin, p. 88.
51. Quarles, p. 185.
52. Id., p. 198.
53. Howard Zinn, *A People's History of the United States* (New York: Harper Colophon Books, 1980), p. 177.
54. Id., p. 215.
55. *Dred Scott v. Sandford*, 19 How. 399, 403; 60 U.S. 663 (1857).
56. Id., p. 410.
57. Id., p. 404-05 (emphasis added).
58. Quarles, p. 240.
59. Id., p. 242.
60. Id., p. 187.
61. Terry Eastland and William J. Bennett, *Counting by Race* (New York: Basic Books, Inc., Publishers, 1979), p. 41 and 26.
62. Id., p. 47.
63. Id., p. 51.
64. Id., p. 54.
65. Id., p. 56.
66. Id., p. 55.
67. Harry V. Jaffa, "The Union Forever Meant the Downfall of Slavery," *Washington Times* (April 21, 1986), p. 6M.

68. Id.
69. McPherson, *The Struggle for Equality*, p. 221.
70. Brief for the United States of America as Amicus Curiae, *Wygant v. Jackson Board of Education*, 54 U.S.L.W. 4479 (U.S. May 20, 1986)(filed June, 1985), p. 15-16.
71. McPherson, *The Struggle for Equality*, p. 346.
72. Id., p. 302.
73. Higgs, p. 7.
74. Myrdal, p. 228.
75. Blaustein and Zangrando, p. 223-24.
76. Id., p. 224-25.
77. Eastland and Bennett, p. 62.
78. Brief for the United States, p. 11.
79. Gerald Gunther, *Cases and Materials on Constitutional Law* (Mineola, N.Y.: The Foundation Press, Inc., 1975), p. 901.
80. Id., p. 902.
81. Eastland and Bennett, p. 65.
82. Brief for Appellants, p. 94.
83. Morris Abram, "Affirmative Action: Fair Shakers and Social Engineers," *Harvard Law Review*, vol. 99, p. 1315 (1986).
84. James J. McPherson, *The Abolitionist Legacy* (Princeton, NJ: Princeton University Press, 1975), p. 35-36.
85. Id., p. 97.

3

The Triumph of Opportunity

The Civil War ended slavery, but also triggered a new, even more difficult struggle to overcome the vestiges of slavery and ensure for blacks a realistic opportunity to participate in the American system on an equal basis.

Given the heady prospects for civil rights following the Civil War, few could predict that the struggle for equal opportunity would require a full century. After all, the political mechanisms guaranteeing equality of rights were fully in place within a few years after the war's conclusion. Indeed, the political reforms of the Reconstruction era prompted Emerson to describe America as the quintessence of individual liberty, providing

> [o]pportunity of civil rights, of education, of personal power, and not less of wealth; doors wide open . . . [in] invitation to every nation, to every race and skin, . . . hospitality of fair field and equal laws to all. Let them compete, and success to the strongest, the wisest, and the best.[1]

But despite America's renewed commitment to the principles of civil rights, an enormous challenge remained. As Frederick Douglass ruminated,

> The real question is whether American justice, American liberty, American civilization, American law and American Christianity can be made to include and protect alike and forever all American citizens. . . . It is whether this great nation shall conquer its prejudices, rise to the dignity of its professions and proceed in the sublime course of truth and liberty.[2]

But as Garrison warned, any hope for fulfilling this civil rights vision during the post-war era would require constant vigilance. With the removal of federal troops and the fading national concern over the plight of the former slaves a decade after the war's conclusion, the freedmen were once again at the mercy of their former enslavers.

The freedmen—uneducated and unskilled in economic and political

31

affairs by virtue of past deprivations—were ill-equipped to meet this challenge and in no position to exploit the political mechanisms newly available to them. The abolitionists, their political agenda accomplished with the passage of the civil rights amendments, were unable to agree upon any further positive strategy for the post-abolition era. The quest for civil rights thus faced its second great crisis.

Once again, the advocates of civil rights turned introspective. They recognized, as historian James McPherson recounts, that real opportunity for blacks "would come only with the acquisition of education, skills, property, and the values of the Protestant ethic, and this could not be done overnight."[3] Voicing this perception, Douglass predicted that when blacks constituted "a class of men noted for enterprise, industry, economy, and success, we shall no longer have any trouble in the matter of civil and political rights."[4]

But as the advocates of civil rights were struggling to craft a new agenda, the Southern white supremacists seized the opportunity to renew their efforts to thwart black progress, by means of a sweeping assortment of deprivations that would make the earlier Black Codes seem mild by comparison. Their first victories were won in the Supreme Court, which took an extremely restrictive view of the recent constitutional amendments, thereby largely abdicating the critical role assigned to the judicial branch as the ultimate guardian of civil rights. In the *Slaughter-House Cases*, for instance, the Court limited the scope of the Fourteenth Amendment so as to essentially preclude the vindication of economic rights that were so critical to black progress. By a 5-4 majority, the Court upheld an exclusive state-imposed slaughterhouse monopoly that severly limited entrepreneurial opportunities in that trade. Justice Field, one of the dissenters, denounced the opinion, "for by it the right of free labor, one of the most sacred and imprescriptible rights of man, is violated."[5] Although another dissenter, Justice Swayne, expressed the "hope that the consequences to follow may prove less serious and far-reaching than the minority fear they will be,"[6] the Court's decision cleared the way for extensive economic regulation that would virtually negate an important facet of the Fourteenth Amendment's promise of equal opportunity for all citizens—a promise that remains unfulfilled today.

Fortified by the Supreme Court's narrow interpretation of the new civil rights protections, the supremacists set out once again to preserve their feudal society by formally assigning blacks to an inferior status. A principal and ongoing vehicle in establishing white supremacy was to secure complete control over Southern governments by nullifying black voting rights. The supremacists contrived sophisticated mechanisms—such as property and literacy requirements and poll taxes, with "grandfather clauses" to exempt whites—that were racially neutral in appearance but explicitly racist in intent and effect. Further, the Democratic Party—nominally a private institution but whose endorsement was tantamount to election in the South—established primaries open only to whites. These mechanisms combined to severly restrict black participation in Southern politics.[7]

Upon securing control over the states' political machinery, the supremacists could implement their objectives at will. At first, they relied upon persuasion and peer pressure to convince Southern landowners to limit employment opportunities and restrict wages. But "[d]espite these admonitions," observes Jennifer Roback, professor of economics at George Mason University, "white employers vigorously competed with one another for black labor."[8] Recognizing that a competitive labor market provided powerful economic disincentives to discrimination, the supremacists soon resorted to coercion through law. As Robert Higgs explains, "[t]he fountainhead of effective discrimination lay in the governments of the Southern states, counties, and cities, where the racial monopoly of politics allowed the hostile whites to treat the blacks as they pleased."[9] The resulting laws, known as "Jim Crow," are described by Professor Roback as "attempts to enforce a labor-market cartel among white employers that could not be enforced in any other way."[10]

Like the Black Codes before them, the early Jim Crow laws constituted a pervasive, interlocking system of economic restraints. During this period, four principal varieties of laws combined to restrict mobility and frustrate competition. The first type was "contract enforcement" laws, which severely limited the times during which laborers could seek new employment. The second type, vagrancy laws, discouraged mobility by making unemployment unlawful. The third, "emigrant-agent" laws, restricted the activities of labor recruiters.[11] The fourth variety, known as "convict leasing" or "debt peonage," imprisoned blacks for debts and furnished them to employers who would assume their obligations in return for their labor until the debts were re-paid.[12] The Jim Crow laws thus represented a rather transparent attempt to guarantee a stable, servile, and inexpensive supply of labor akin to slavery, relegating blacks to a separate, subordinate caste.

This system left precious little room for black progress and few opportunities for black leadership. What progress and leadership was possible was provided primarily by Booker T. Washington, who, for a quarter-century, safeguarded the flickering flame of civil rights while championing self-improvement among blacks.

Born a slave in Virginia, Washington was educated at the Hampton Institute, and founded the Tuskegee Institute in 1881 to teach work skills to blacks. Upon Frederick Douglass' death, Washington became the leading spokesman for blacks.[13] Washington's introspective approach paralleled that of Douglass—incremental progress through hard work and education. He emphasized that blacks must look to themselves if they wished to improve their condition:

> [P]rogress in the enjoyment of all the privileges that will come to us must be the result of severe and constant struggle rather than of artificial forcing. No race that has anything to contribute to the markets of the world is long in any degree ostracized.[14]

Recognizing that Southern political processes were unavailable to blacks, Washington focused instead upon the vestiges of capitalism that managed to survive in that feudal system, and urged blacks to develop the one commodity with which they could bargain for future gains—their labor. Washington reasoned that in the bleak political environment of the post–Civil War South, economic development would invariably produce a greater degree of individual freedom and autonomy than would political demands.

In order to pursue this strategy openly and vigorously, Washington reached a critical accomodation with the white supremacists. In his famous "Atlanta Address" in 1895, he proclaimed that "[i]n all things purely social we can be as separate as the five fingers, and yet one as the hand in all things essential to mutual progress."[15] Washington's imagery summarized a compromise that was tolerable to many supremacists—a tacit acceptance of social segregation in exchange for an opportunity for economic development. As Myrdal later summarized it, Washington was "willing to flatter the Southern Whites and be harsh toward the Negroes—*if* the Negroes were only allowed to work undisturbed with their white friends for education and business."[16] Though Washington took pains not to threaten the supremacists or challenge their superior social status, his message contained an implicit warning:

> We shall constitute one-third and more of the ignorance and crime of the South, or one-third of its intelligence and progress; we shall contribute one-third to the business and industrial prosperity of the South, or we shall prove a veritable body of death, stagnating, depressing, retarding every effort to advance the body politic.[17]

Faced with this grim alternative, many supremacists came to at least tolerate Washington's endeavors.

Though Washington would later be vilified by civil rights advocates such as W.E.B. DuBois for his concessions to the white supremacists, history suggests that Washington's approach was an effective one. Myrdal correctly observed that Washington's "main motive ... was accomodation *for a price*."[18] Though constrained by the stifling subjugation of blacks that characterized the period in which he lived, he managed to secure the trust of many of the supremacists, and in so doing opened a slight bit the window of opportunity that the Jim Crow laws were intended to shut.

Indeed, considering the obstacles they faced, blacks scored impressive gains during this period in terms of both economic and educational growth, laying the foundation for future advances. Proving Washington's point that the market provides disincentives to discrimination, intense competition for black labor continued despite the most pervasive state-imposed restrictions. This competition induced increases in crop shares for tenant workers from a one-twelfth share in 1865 to a half share—along with housing, fuel, and garden plots—only a decade later.[19] Overall, blacks increased their per capita incomes by 300% during the first half century of freedom.[20] Blacks flexed their burgeoning economic muscle through boycotts of white businesses across the South between 1892-1907,[21] presaging the widespread and effective use of this technique fifty years later. Thus, despite the best efforts of the white supremacists, many blacks effectively parlayed the demand for labor and their growing status as consumers to their advantage during the Jim Crow period. Indeed, some black leaders looked upon the Jim Crow coercions as a challenge that would inspire blacks to overcome the odds they faced. The Rev. Richard Henry Boyd, president of the Nashville Negro Business League, was among those who confidently claimed that "[t]hese discriminations are only blessings in disguise. They stimulate and encourage rather than cower and humiliate the true, ambitious, self-determined Negro."[22]

Many blacks managed to overcome state-imposed obstacles to prosper educationally during this period as well. The American Missionary Association and other groups established hundreds of schools serving tens of thousands of black students.[23] The results of the emphasis on education were impressive—between 1865 and 1892, the number of black newspapers increased from two to 154; attorneys from two to 250; physicians from three to 749; and the rate of black illiteracy declined from 80% to 45%.[24] Even Washington's chief detractor, W.E.B. DuBois, conceded that "above the sneers of the critics" stands "one crushing rejoinder"—in a single generation, the missionary schools produced "thirty thousand black teachers in the South" and "wiped out the illiteracy of the majority of black people of the land."[25] These efforts, DuBois concluded, were "the salvation of the South and the Negro. Had it not been for the Negro school and college, the Negro would, to all intents and purposes, have been driven back to slavery."[26]

Clearly, Washington's program engendered progress at a time when prospects for blacks were particularly bleak. The emphasis on economic and educational growth in the midst of oppression helped countless blacks overcome illiteracy and poverty to acquire some degree of self-esteem and control over their own destinies.

Had these efforts continued unabated, blacks over time could have achieved equal economic standing with whites despite the deprivations of the Jim Crow era. George C. White, a black congressman from North Carolina, argued this proposition in 1901:

> I want to submit a brief recipe for the solution of the so-called American negro problem. He asks no special favors, but simply demands that he be given the same chance for existence, for earning a livelihood, for raising himself in the scales of manhood and womanhood that are accorded to kindred nationalities.[27]

But the supremacists, keenly cognizant of the impressive gains by blacks despite pervasive barriers, were determined to frustrate even these basic aspirations. Buttressed by the ideology of Social Darwinism, whose notions of Anglo-Saxon superiority were gripping virtually the entire nation, the supremacists devised new methods to systematically arrest further economic and educational development, restrict mobility, and remove any real protection of property rights for blacks, thereby thwarting the proposed scenario for upward social mobility.[28]

Civil rights deprivations assumed even more virulent forms than before as the supremacists determined that blacks were unfit for even the most peripheral contacts with whites. "Separate but equal" laws were enacted as measures to prevent social contamination of the "superior race" by blacks. These new discriminations were sanctioned by the Supreme Court in *Plessy v. Ferguson*, the most pernicious and disastrous decision for civil rights since *Dred Scott* forty years earlier. In *Plessy*, the Court retreated fully from the principle of constitutional color-blindness, substituting instead a "reasonableness" standard that is still invoked today to sustain the current breed of state-imposed discrimination. The Court held that statutes requiring separate railroad accomodations for blacks are "within the competency of the state legislatures in the exercise of their police power."[29] The equal rights secured after years of bloody Civil War were all but abandoned in Justice Brown's opinion:

> So far, then, as a conflict with the Fourteenth Amendment is concerned, the case reduces itself to the question whether the statute of Louisiana is a *reasonable* regulation, and with respect to this there must be a large discretion on the part of the legislature.[30]

Justice John M. Harlan dissented, standing alone in maintaining fidelity to the principles of civil rights. "In respect of civil rights, common to all citizens," he declared, the Constitution does not "permit any public authority to know the race of those entitled to be protected in the enjoyment of such rights."[31] Harlan proceeded to set out the analytical framework that would be championed by all sincere civil rights advocates in the years ahead:

> Our Constitution is color-blind, and neither knows nor tolerates classes among citizens. In respect of civil rights, all citizens are equal before the law. . . . The law regards man as man, and takes no account of . . . his color when his civil rights as guaranteed by the supreme law of the land are involved. It is therefore to be regretted that this high tribunal, the final expositor of the fundamental law of the land, has reached the conclusion that it is competent for a state to regulate the enjoyment by citizens of their civil rights solely upon the basis of race.[32]

Tragically, Harlan was the sole dissenter, and his views, though in accord with the letter and spirit of the Fourteenth Amendment, remain a minority position on the Court today. Predictably, *Plessy* opened the floodgates to segregation. In the two decades following this infamous decision, the Southern states imposed segregation in virtually every public facility, from railroads and streetcars to schools and prisons.[33]

But the supremacists were not satisfied with extinguishing economic opportunity and social interaction. They quickly turned their attention to education, passing statutes such as Kentucky's Day Law in 1904, mandating segregation in private schools, which the supremacists viewed as organs for integration.[34] The Supreme Court upheld such a statute in *Berea College v. Kentucky*, in which it sustained as a proper application of the State's regulatory authority over corporations a $1,000 fine against a school that violated the segregation law. Justice Harlan again dissented, charging that "the statute is an arbitrary invasion of the rights of liberty and property guaranteed by the Fourteenth Amendment against hostile state action, and is, therefore, void."[35] He plaintively queried his countrymen,

> Have we become so inoculated with prejudice of race that an American government, professedly based on the principles of freedom, and charged with the protection of all citizens alike, can make distinctions between such citizens in the matter of their voluntary meeting for innocent purposes simply because of their respective races?[36]

Once again, the deprivation of civil rights was nearly complete, and the need for stronger action on the part of civil rights advocates became increasingly apparent. The doors were now firmly shut to the approach advocated by Booker T. Washington. An alternative agenda, geared toward confronting rather than working within the new barriers, was clearly necessary.

This challenge produced not one, but two distinct approaches, initiating a split in the civil rights movement that would re-emerge in the 1960s. The first approach embraced the traditional principles of civil rights, but set aside Washington's exclusive focus on self-improvement in favor of a frontal assault upon the *system* of discrimination. This new strategy was marked by the emergence of W.E.B. DuBois, whose classic work entitled *The Souls of Black Folk* in 1903 established the basic framework for the civil rights movement for the next sixty years.

DuBois concisely identified the seminal issue at the outset: "The problem of the twentieth century is the problem of the color-line."[37] This issue, explained DuBois, presented the critical question of "how far differences of race . . . will hereafter be made the basis of denying to over half the world the right of sharing to their utmost ability the opportunities and principles of modern civilization."[38]

At the outset, DuBois endeavored to distinguish his prescription from Washington's. He denounced Washington's "Atlanta Compromise," charging that blacks had "surrendered their civil and political rights" in exchange for "larger chances of economic development."[39] DuBois contended that such a strategy was woefully insufficient. "Is it possible," he asked rhetorically, "that nine millions of men can make effective progress in economic lines if they are deprived of political rights, made a servile caste, and allowed only the most meagre chance for developing their exceptional men?"[40]

But although DuBois criticized Washington harshly and incessantly, their differences turned far more on strategy than philosophy. For DuBois—though he would later associate himself with the Socialist Party—firmly established himself in *Souls* as an intellectual heir to Paine, Garrison, Douglass, and the other leading civil rights advocates preceding him. Invoking the mantle of the traditional civil rights vision, DuBois declared, "There are to-day no truer exponents of the pure human spirit of the Declaration of Independence than the American Negroes."[41] Accordingly, his goal was to secure civil rights for blacks so they could fulfil their individual aspirations:

> Above our modern socialism, and out of the worship of the mass, must persist and evolve that higher individualism which the centres of culture protect; there must come a loftier respect for the sovereign human soul that seeks to know itself and the world about it; that seeks a freedom for expansion and self-development. . . .[42]

In stark contrast to DuBois' classical civil rights approach emerged the separatist movement of Marcus Garvey. His Universal Negro Improvement Association rejected the emphasis DuBois placed on individualism during this period, appealing instead to racial pride and purity. Garvey urged blacks to reject American society altogether and to form a separate nation in Africa. Although his strategy implicitly embraced the very "color line" that DuBois decried, Garvey echoed both Washington and DuBois by rejecting preferential treatment and demanding only an equal chance to progress and prosper. "[W]hen of our own initiative we strike out to build industries, governments, and ultimately empires," Garvey argued, "then and only then will we as a race prove to our Creator and to man in general that we are fit to survive and capable of shaping our own destiny."[43]

The separatist movement collapsed as Garvey became embroiled in legal problems which culminated in his deportation in 1927.[44] Even apart from Garvey's legal difficulties, however, most blacks rejected separatism in and of itself. Separatism, Gunnar Myrdal observed, is self-defeating, because by stressing racial differences, it provides "the caste system a certain moral sanction."[45] By rejecting separatism, Myrdal explained, "Negroes show . . . that they have not lost their belief that ultimately the American Creed will come out on top."[46]

The course charted by DuBois included none of the cynicism that induced the demise of Garvey's separatism. Blacks, he contended, had already established their moral fitness. DuBois believed it was time to challenge the American system to provide the basic rights with whose protection it was charged. "We shall not be satisfied to take one jot or title less than our full manhood rights," he exhorted. "We claim for ourselves every single right that belongs to a freeborn American, political, civil and social."[47]

DuBois and his supporters recognized that concerted action was essential in securing these rights. William Lloyd Garrison, Jr. urged that the time had come for "colored people to organize for lawful self-defense and for white lovers of liberty to stand up for equal rights." The "recrudescence of slavery," he warned, "must be met with the undaunted purpose that the abolitionists displayed, for the conflict is the same irrepressible one."[48]

This spirit animated the first meeting of twenty-nine black intellectuals in Niagra Falls in 1905 to organize a movement to agitate for civil rights.[49] The "Niagra movement" led to the founding four years later of the National Association for the Advancement of Colored People (NAACP). DuBois was a key organizer and went on to edit its monthly publication, *The Crisis*, for the next twenty-four years.[50] Another founder, Oswald Garrison Villard, described the NAACP's mission as one of action rather than accomodation. It was obvious, Villard remarked, that the race problem "will not work itself out by the mere lapse of time or by the operation of education. There is only one remedy—that the colored people shall have every one of the privileges and rights of American citizens."[51]

The NAACP adopted a clear agenda for achieving these objectives. Its program called for a color-blind society—"[t]he abolition of color-hyphenation and the substitution of straight Americanism,"—through equal voting rights, equal educational opportunity, fair trials, the right to sit on juries, anti-lynching laws, equal treatment on public carriers, equal access to public services for which citizens were taxed, and equal employment opportunities.[52] Like the civil rights advocates before them—and in contrast to the separatists—the NAACP firmly committed itself to the original civil rights vision.

But the NAACP's program was extremely ambitious, particularly in the context of an almost total negation of the rights of blacks in the early part of the twentieth century. The Wilson administration was particularly noxious, initiating numerous new discriminations including segregation in federal employment.[53] Nonetheless, the NAACP and its allies set out to methodically challenge in every available forum the pervasive discriminatory apparatus with which they were confronted.

Early progress during this period was stymied by the Depression, and a plea for economic relief temporarily supplanted the quest for opportunity. The Depression fundamentally altered the dominant view of the proper role of the state in society. As Gunnar Myrdal would observe, some tension had always existed between the American ideals of liberty and equality, but now "[e]quality is slowly winning. The New Deal during the 'thirties was a landslide."[54] By illustration, before 1929, spending at all levels of government had never exceeded 12% of national income; but by 1933, it had increased to 20%.[55]

Notwithstanding the need for short-term relief, the potential for a perpetual underclass rendered complacent by the welfare state did not escape the civil rights advocates. Even Franklin Roosevelt cautioned in 1935 that "[c]ontinued dependency upon relief induces a spirtual and moral disintegration, fundamentally destructive to the national fiber."[56] The NAACP declined to succumb to the lure of government paternalism, pursuing instead its tenacious challenges against such deprivations as segregation, lynching, debt peonage, and disenfranchisement.[57]

Prospects for advancement were necessarily bleak during the Depression, but fundamental issues of civil rights were suddenly thrust to the forefront of national attention for the first time since Reconstruction by the rise of Adolph Hitler. Faced with the challenge of Hitler's explicitly racist ideology, America responded by invoking its sacred ideals of liberty and democracy—what Myrdal described as "the ideological foundation of national morale."[58] America was thus forced to confront the tragic inconsistency that would give rise to Myrdal's insightful *An American Dilemma* in 1944—the nation's professed devotion to the American Creed, standing in stark juxtaposition to the wholesale violations of that Creed by its subordination of blacks. Despite this contradiction, Myrdal observed that the "liberal Creed is adhered to by every American. The unanimity around, and the explicitness of, this Creed is the great wonder of America."[59] Yet, while blacks subscribed to the Creed, they were systematically excluded from its benefits. Myrdal urged the civil rights movement to overcome this hypocrisy by invoking "the great Abolitionist tradition, taking its stand on the American Constitution and fighting for equality in justice and for suffrage, keeping alive the unabridged ideals of the American Creed."[60] A sincere commitment to the principles of civil rights, Myrdal urged, was the only means to resolve the American dilemma.

Thus did World War II inspire a national soul-searching that provided the greatest opportunity for the expansion of civil rights since the Civil War. Even then, however, setbacks occurred. In the midst of a war pitting the ideals of individualism versus totalitarianism, the Roosevelt administration sanctioned a blatant denial of civil rights through the internment of American citizens of Japanese ancestry. This shocking betrayal of basic American principles was immediately challenged in the Supreme Court, which promptly demonstrated that even a professedly "liberal" court can find excuses to depart from the fundamental rule that government must not violate rights on the basis of race. In *Korematsu v. United States*, Justice Hugo Black wrote for a 6-3 majority that the exclusion was permissible as a "temporary" military measure, overlooking the fact that in times of war civil rights are most vulnerable and therefore require even greater protection. As in *Plessy*, the Court rejected the absolute nature of the Constitution's prohibition against race-based government action, instead according government wide discretion to nullify civil rights in the "public interest."

But the three dissenters, arguing that the exception proved the rule, were not persuaded that ill-conceived military exigencies justified what Justice Murphy termed "one of the most sweeping and complete deprivations of constitutional rights in the history of this nation."[61] Justice Jackson, a fellow dissenter, focused upon the enduring effects attending any compromise of the absolute principle of constitutional color-blindness, warning with noteworthy prescience that

> a judicial construction . . . that will sustain this [internment] order is a far more subtle blow to liberty than the promulgation of the order itself. . . . [O]nce a judicial opinion rationalizes the Constitution to show that [it] sanctions such an order, the Court for all time has validated the principle of racial discrimination. . . . The principle then lies about like a loaded weapon ready

for the hand of any authority that can bring forward a plausible claim of an urgent need.[62]

Of course, the loaded gun that Justice Jackson described has since been fired time and again, and always with the same tragic results. *Korematsu* thus joined the long line of decisions in which the judicial branch abdicated its central role in the protection of civil rights, and foreshadowed more recent decisions that rely upon equally questionable rationalizations in departing from the principle of color-blindness.

Fortunately, blacks fared better during World War II than did the Japanese, seizing the opportunity to challenge America to apply its professed ideals to eradicate the color line. The effort to extract concessions in return for war support was spearheaded by union activist A. Philip Randolph, who choreographed a massive march on Washington in 1941 to dramatize the plight of blacks. Randolph came quickly to the point of the protest:

> What have the Negroes to fight for? What's the difference between Hitler and that "cracker" Talmadge from Georgia? Why has a man got to be Jim-Crowed to die for democracy . . . ? [I]f freedom and equality are not vouchsafed for the peoples of color, the war for democracy will not be won.[63]

Randolph delivered a series of eight demands, at whose core was a plea for color-blindness through the "the abrogation of every law which makes a distinction in treatment between citizens based on religion, creed, color, or national origin."[64] If these demands were not met, blacks threatened to withhold their support for the war effort, thereby jeopardizing America's claim to moral supremacy in the war against Hitler.

Roosevelt responded quickly, issuing an Executive Order prohibiting employment discrimination by the federal government or defense contractors.[65] President Truman followed his predecessor's lead, declaring that "there is no justifiable reason for discrimination because of . . . color," and resolving that America's "immediate task is to remove the last remnants of the barriers which stand between millions of our citizens and their birthright."[66]

Truman appointed a Committee on Civil Rights, whose report, entitled *To Secure These Rights*, concluded that blacks were systematically deprived of four basic rights: the right to safety and security, to citizenship and its privileges, to freedom of conscience and expression, and to equality of opportunity.[67] The committee echoed Myrdal's prescription for the American dilemma:

> We have no further justification for a broad and immediate program than the need to reaffirm our faith in traditional American morality. The pervasive

gap between our aims and what we actually do is creating a kind of moral dry rot which eats away at the emotional and rational bases of democratic beliefs.[68]

The committee report reflected a burgeoning national consensus that developed during the war—that blacks, who had fought against fascism in defense of American ideals, were entitled to have those ideals honored. The growing spectre of communism and its subordination of individual rights underscored the necessity for making good on that promise. Truman emphasized this concern in 1948, remarking that "the democratic way of life is being challenged all over the world. Democracy's answer to the challenge of totalitarianism is its promise of equal rights and equal opportunity for all mankind."[69] The Republican platform that same year also unequivocally attached itself to the cause of civil rights:

One of the basic principles of this Republic is the equality of all individuals in their right to life, liberty and the pursuit of happiness. This principle is enunciated in the Declaration of Independence and embodied in the Constitution of the United States; it was vindicated in battle and became the cornerstone of the Republic. This right of equal opportunity to work and to advance in life should never be limited in any individual because of race.[70]

Thus, in the aftermath of enormous conflict, the civil rights movement had once again firmly established a core of popular consensus. The questions now confronting the movement were how far it could go and how it would get there.

The movement had learned from past experience the hard lesson that consensus could be fleeting; hence, it must move rapidly to achieve substantive gains. A large part of the movement's emphasis was placed on securing victories through the courts, for while enormous resistance continued in Congress, the judicial climate appeared increasingly hospitable. The goal in the judicial arena was clear: to reverse *Plessy v. Ferguson* and its dreaded "separate but equal" doctrine, and to replace it with an absolute rule of constitutional color-blindness consistent with the purposes of the Fourteenth Amendment.

The strategy proved remarkably successful. One by one the barriers to civil rights began to fall, and the Court moved step by step toward the ultimate goal of constitutional color-blindness. In *Cassell v. State of Texas*, for instance, the Supreme Court struck down a law limiting the number of blacks on juries on the basis of "proportional representation." The Court mandated equality of *opportunity* to sit on a jury, while emphatically precluding any preordained equality in *result*. Justice Felix Frankfurter explained that "[t]he prohibition of the Constitution against discrimination does not require in and of itself the presence of a Negro on a jury. But neither is it satisfied by Negro representation arbitrarily limited to one." Instead, "[t]he basis of selection cannot consciously take color into account. Such is the command of the Constitution."[71]

Most of the legal focus during the 1950s centered on state-imposed discrimination in education, revisiting issues that had been decided adversely earlier in the century in *Berea College* and similar holdings. This time, the civil rights advocates found a far more receptive Court. In *McLaurin v. Oklahoma State Regents for Higher Education*, the Court swept aside rules requiring a black student to sit in a separate row in classes and at a separate table in the library and cafeteria. The Court was not persuaded by arguments that the rule was permissible as an expression of social realities— i.e., that even absent the rules, the black student would be treated differently by his fellow students, and hence that striking down the rule would not necessarily produce any different outcome. Instead, the Court held that the Constitution requires equal opportunity, even if equal results will not necessarily follow. Chief Justice Vinson, writing for a unanimous Court, declared that "[t]he Fourteenth Amendment precludes differences in treatment by the state based upon race."[72] Vinson conceded "[t]he removal of the state restrictions will not necessarily abate individual and group predilections, prejudices and choices"; but ruled that the Constitution forbids the state from depriving a person of "the *opportunity* to secure acceptance by his fellow students on his own merits."[73] The Court's decision demonstrated that after more than eighty years, the Fourteenth Amendment's great promise for civil rights was finally being realized.

The most important triumph in the courts came with the complete repudiation of the notion that enforced separation could ever satisfy the constitutional requirement of equal protection of the laws. The question was presented in *Brown v. Board of Education*, in which schoolchildren in Topeka, Kansas were limited to certain schools on the basis of race. Delivering the momentous oral argument was Thurgood Marshall, veteran of numerous civil rights court battles and general counsel for the NAACP. The NAACP's brief, which comprised perhaps the most brilliant and comprehensive statement of the development and philosophical underpinnings of the civil rights vision, set out the seminal issue presented in the case:

> The importance to our American democracy of the substantive question can hardly be overstated. The question is whether a nation founded on the proposition that "all men are created equal" is honoring its commitments to grant "due process of law" and "the equal protection of the laws" . . . when it, or one of its constituent states, confers or denies benefits on the basis of color or race.[74]

The brief traced the evolution of civil rights from their origins in natural law as interpreted by Jefferson and Locke through the ratification of the Fourteenth Amendment. The framers of that amendment, the NAACP brief demonstrated, "were formulating a constitutional provision setting broad standards for determination of the relationship of the state to the individual."[75] Their primary intent, the brief emphasized, was to "prohibit all state action predicated upon race or color."[76] Drawing from the unambiguous history of the quest for civil rights in America, the NAACP could confidently proclaim "[t]hat the Constitution is color blind is our dedicated belief."[77]

The Court agreed with the NAACP's argument and struck down the segregation in a unanimous opinion by Chief Justice Warren. The Court declared that education, "where the state has undertaken to provide it, is a right which must be made available to all on equal terms."[78] Although the Court stopped short of embracing the absolute view of constitutional color-blindness pressed by the NAACP, it unequivocally consigned the pernicious race-conscious doctrine of *Plessy* to its long-overdue demise.

Fortified by its triumphs in the courts, the civil rights movement expanded its focus to include mass protests and political pressure designed to produce additional legal bulwarks against discrimination. This shift in strategy coincided with the emergence of a new national leader who personified the civil rights vision. Martin Luther King, Jr., a 27-year-old Baptist minister, was catapulted to prominence by his response to an incident of discrimination that had become commonplace in the South. On December 1, 1955, Mrs. Rosa Parks, a black woman, was arrested for violating a Montgomery ordinance by refusing to move to the rear of a public bus for the benefit of white passengers. For Dr. King, the incident was a microcosm of the battle for civil rights. Rosa Parks symbolized far more than a tired woman engaged in a momentary protest—as King viewed it, "[s]he was anchored to that seat by the accumulated indignities of days gone by and the boundless aspirations of generations yet unborn."[79] The remarkably successful public transit boycott that followed, organized and inspired by King, launched an ambitious effort to capture the minds and hearts of the American public through non-violent protest.

King was an intellectual heir to Locke and Jefferson, Garrison and Douglass, Washington and DuBois. As did all his predecessors, King consistently drew upon the Declaration of Independence as the highest expression of his civil rights vision. The Declaration provided the cornerstone of King's famous "I Have a Dream" speech on the steps of the Lincoln Memorial in 1963. King's dream was of the realization of the Declaration's central premise that "[a]ll men are created equal" and endowed "with certain inalienable rights." King valued this passage for its universalism, but also because it affirmed "that there are certain basic rights that are neither confirmed by nor derived from the state." This principle provided the critical characteristic that distinguished America "from systems of government which make the state an end within itself."[80] Based upon this understanding, King firmly aligned himself with "what is best in the American dream," toward the goal of "bringing our nation back to the great wells of democracy which were dug deep by the founding fathers in their formulation of the Constitution and the Declaration of Independence."[81]

In Martin Luther King, the civil rights vision had found a forceful proponent who was faithful to its traditional principles. Indeed, King's foremost contribution was in keeping the civil rights vision on track in the face of intense pressure toward violence and revolution. The leading proponent of the militant strategy was Malcolm X, whose message to his followers was explicitly racial: "[W]e all have in common the greatest binding tie we could have . . . we all are *black* people. . . . Our enemy is the *white man!*"[82] This philosophy formed the basis of the "black power" slogan popularized by Stokely Carmichael and other black separatists. The separatists' strategy was extremely radical, calling for "reallocation of land, of money."[83] While preaching black pride, Carmichael rejected the individualism upon which the traditional civil rights vision was based, declaring "[t]he society we wish to build . . . is not a capitalist one. . . . When we urge that black money go into black pockets, we mean the communal pocket."[84]

This injection of race-consciousness into the national debate alarmed King and his allies because it threatened to divide blacks and alienate white sympathizers upon the very threshold of victory. Roy Wilkins warned that

> [f]or the first time . . . there emerges what seems to be a difference in goals. Heretofore there were some differences in methods and emphasis but none in ultimate goals. The end was always to be the inclusion of the American Negro, without racial discrimination, as a Full Fledged equal in all phases of American citizenship. [85]

Likewise, King rejected calls for "black power" as "racism in reverse." He emphasized that "[w]e must never seek power exclusively for the Negro, but the sharing of power with the white people. Any other course is exchanging one form of tyranny for another."[86] Wilkins denounced racism by blacks even more vehemently, charging that "black power" constitutes "a reverse Mississippi, a reverse Hitler, a reverse Ku Klux Klan. . . . We of the NAACP will have none of this. We have fought it too long."[87] King and his allies thus fully appreciated the necessity of promoting a universally vested interest in civil rights, and were careful to cultivate the burgeoning renewal of commitment to civil rights by mainstream America. Of whites, King argued that "their destiny is tied up with our destiny and their freedom is inextricably bound to our freedom,"[88] recognizing that history had so vividly demonstrated time and again that civil rights are tenuous if they are not held equally by all.

King's advocacy of a color-blind society was particularly passionate since his comprehension of the nature of racism was so keen. King observed that

> [r]acism is a philosophy based on contempt for life. . . . If a man asserts that another man, because of his race, is not good enough to have a job equal to his, . . . or to attend school with him, or to live next door to him, he is by implication affirming that that man does not deserve to exist . . . because his existence is corrupt and defective.[89]

This understanding provided the foundation for King's uncompromising quest for a society in which race was irrelevant; in which individuals "will not be judged by the color of their skin but by the content of their character."[90] Accordingly, the civil rights movement's ultimate goal was to lift the barriers to an integrated society; to ensure once and for all equal opportunities for blacks in such areas as education, employment, and housing. As James Farmer of the Congress of Racial Equality explained, the movement's objective was "color-blindness permeat[ing] the land." Integration, he declared, "has been the nation's implicit ideal since America was a glint in Jefferson's eye. It is nothing but Jeffersonian individualism extended to all people."[91]

In practical terms, this objective translated not into forced equality of result, but rather, as Farmer emphasized, the goal of "total freedom of choice . . . throughout American society."[92] Farmer continued,

> What we wish is the freedom of choice which will cause any choice we make to seem truly our own. . . . A person should be able to choose where he wants to live and live there. If he chooses to live in Lovely Lane in Orchard Gardens, he should be able to, if he has the money to swing it. Jim Brown, a thoughtful man and a pretty good fullback, offended some people when he said that he personally wouldn't want to live with whites but that he damned well wanted to know that he could if he did want to. I think he represents the thinking of many Negroes.[93]

Opportunity and choice—not forced equality of result—were the hallmarks of this vision.

Although the white supremacists reacted to the progress of the civil rights movement with increasing violence against people and property, most Americans were at long last prepared to make the promise of civil rights a reality. President Kennedy, reflecting the growing national consensus, responded to Dr. King's Lincoln Memorial address by asking Congress "to make a commitment it has not fully made in this century to the proposition that race has no place in American life or law." The Constitution, he declared, is "color blind," and every American "should have the equal right to develop [his] talent and ability and motivation."[94]

Kennedy's tragic death occurred before he could make good on his promise. But Congress moved swiftly to eradicate discrimination. It passed the Civil Rights Act of 1964, prohibiting discrimination in public accomodations, employment, and any program receiving federal assistance; as well as the Twenty-fourth Amendment and the Voting Rights Act of 1965, prohibiting poll taxes and guaranteeing equal access to the franchise in primary and general elections. Meanwhile, the Supreme Court continued to strike down state-imposed racial barriers such as the pernicious miscegenation laws prohibiting marriages among the races, reiterating once again that the "clear and central purpose of the Fourteenth Amendment was to eliminate all official state sources of invidious racial discrimination in the States."[95]

All of the enactments during this period were directed toward creating a color-blind society, and for the most part provided potentially effective tools with which to pursue that end. The employment provisions of the Civil Rights Act, for instance, were designed to free the labor market of discrimination on the basis of race and other characteristics, while leaving essential market mechanisms intact. This emphasis was critical, since a large share of whatever economic gains had been made by blacks in the century since slavery occurred because the market—to the extent it is free from state-imposed impediments designed to frustrate its operation—discourages discrimination by assigning its costs to the discriminator. As Morris Abram, former vice-chairman of the U.S. Commission on Civil Rights recalls, the civil rights activists understood that "removing all barriers to the exercise of an individual's ability to participate in a free market system is the best possible way to promote justice."[96]

This view was reflected by the framers of the act. The primary sponsor, Senator Hubert H. Humphrey, summarized the act's effect by emphasizing that it "does not limit the employer's freedom to hire, fire, promote, or demote for any reasons—or for no reasons—so long as his action is not based on race."[97] Another sponsor, Senator Thomas Kuchel, emhasized that "the bill . . . is color-blind."[98] Accordingly, subsequent efforts to utilize the act to produce preferential treatment are in conflict with its clearly expressed purposes and principles. As Senator Clark observed, racial "[q]uotas are themselves discriminatory." Fellow Senate sponsor Harrison Williams added rhetorically, "[H]ow can the language of equality favor one race . . . over another? . . . Those who say that equality means favoritism do violence to commonsense."[99] Likewise, Senator Humphrey declared,

[O]ur standard of judgment in the last analysis is not some group's power . . . but an *equal* opportunity for *persons*.

Do you want a society that is nothing but an endless power struggle among organized groups? Do you want a society where there is no place for the independent individual? I don't.[100]

Thus, far from providing yet another rationale for racial decisionmaking, the act was unequivocally designed to move America substantially closer to a goal that had eluded civil rights advocates for two hundred years—a society in which decisions are made on the basis of merit and where "the color of man's skin . . . [is] completely extraneous."[101]

In some respects the Civil Rights Act did not go far enough. The act left largely intact the legacy of the *Slaughter-House Cases*—the power of government to subject voluntary economic activity to such pervasive regulation that it often precludes meaningful opportunities. Indeed, governmental entities were not even covered by the employment provisions of the act until 1972. Morever, by failing to eliminate such federal regulations as minimum wage laws and by mandating equal wages in all cases, the act limited the bargaining power that blacks and immigrant groups had historically exploited to overcome prejudice and obtain entry into the labor market. As University of Massachusetts economics Professor Simon Rottenberg explains, such restrictions as minimum wage and equal pay laws, regardless of how benevolent they appear, "dilute the incentive given employers to employ blacks rather than whites"[102] by mandating the same wages for each, thus allowing employers to indulge racist predilections without bearing the cost that the market would otherwise assign.

But by and large, the Civil Rights Act of 1964 provided an important new weapon by which to advance individual rights. Indeed, it marked the apex of the golden decade in the quest for civil rights, a period in which, as activist Bayard Rustin reflected, "the legal foundations of racism in America were destroyed."[103] Equal opportunity had triumphed.

As with the aftermath of abolitionism a century earlier, the focus of the civil rights movement following the triumph of opportunity would shift to the beneficiaries of the recent gains to consolidate and exploit the newly available opportunities, and to the advocates of civil rights to consider and confront the remaining obstacles. But whatever challenges lay ahead, America could finally draw solace—and pride—in the fact that it was closer than ever before to fulfilling the promise of civil rights for all its citizens.

Notes

1. Nathan Glazer, *Affirmative Discrimination: Ethnic Inequality and Public Policy* (New York: Basic Books, Inc., Publishers, 1975), p. 18.

2. Sorin, p. 119.
3. McPherson, *The Abolitionist Legacy*, p. 79.
4. Id., p. 72.
5. *Slaughter-House Cases*, 83 U.S. 36, 110 (1873) (Field, J., dissenting).
6. Id., p. 130 (Swayne, J., dissenting).
7. C. Vann Woodward, *The Strange Career of Jim Crow*, 2d rev. ed. (New York: Oxford University Press, 1966), p. 83-84.
8. Jennifer Roback, "Southern Labor Law in the Jim Crow Era: Exploitative or Competitive?" *Univ. of Chicago L. Rev.* Vol. 51, p. 1161 (1984).
9. Higgs, p. 134.
10. Roback, p. 1162.
11. Id., p. 1163-64.
12. Myrdal, p. 228-29.
13. Blaustein and Zangrando, p. 288.
14. Id., p. 292.
15. W.E.B. DuBois, *The Souls of Black Folk* (Millwood, N.Y.: Kraus-Thomson Organization Limited, 1973), p. 42.
16. Myrdal, p. 739.
17. Blaustein and Zangrando, p. 291.
18. Myrdal, p. 86.
19. Higgs, p. 49.
20. Id., p. 134.
21. August Meier and Elliott Rudwick, "The Boycott Movement against Jim Crow Streetcars in the South, 1900-1906," in Curtis and Gould, p. 90-92.
22. Id., p. 110.
23. McPherson, *The Abolitionist Legacy*, p. 144-45.
24. Id., p. 222.
25. Id., p. 223.
26. Id., p. 160.
27. Blaustein and Zangrando, p. 316.
28. Higgs, p. 11.
29. *Plessy v. Ferguson*, 163 U.S. 537, 544 (1896).
30. Id., p. 550 (emphasis added).
31. Id, p. 554 (Harlan, J., dissenting).
32. Id., p. 559.
33. Eastland and Bennett, p. 83-84.
34. McPherson, *The Abolitionist Legacy*, p. 253.
35. *Berea College v. Kentucky*, 211 U.S. 45, 67 (Harlan, J., dissenting).
36. Id., p. 69.
37. DuBois, p. 13.
38. John E. Fleming, *The Lengthening Shadow of Slavery* (Washington, D.C.: Howard University Press, 1976), p. 83.
39. DuBois, p. 13.
40. Id., p. 51.
41. Id., p. 11.
42. Id., p. 108.
43. Myrdal, p. 746.
44. Blaustein and Zangrando, p. 343.
45. Myrdal, p. 798, n."a."
46. Id., p. 799.

47. Fleming, p. 81-82.
48. McPherson, *The Abolitionist Legacy*, p. 372.
49. Myrdal, p. 742.
50. Blaustein and Zangrando, p. 324.
51. McPherson, *The Abolitionist Legacy*, p. 299.
52. Blaustein and Zangrando, p. 338.
53. Eastland and Bennett, p. 88.
54. Myrdal, p. 9.
55. Milton and Rose Friedman, *Free to Choose* (New York: Harcourt Brace Javanovich, 1980), p. 92.
56. Henry Hazlitt, *Man vs. the Welfare State* (New Rochelle, N.Y.: Arlington House, 1969), p. 57-58.
57. Myrdal, p. 820.
58. Id., p. 5.
59. Id., p. 13.
60. Id., p. 854.
61. *Korematsu v. United States*, 323 U.S. 214, 235 (1944) (Murphy, J., dissenting).
62. Id., p. 245-46 (Jackson, J., dissenting).
63. Eastland and Bennett, p. 108.
64. Id.
65. Id.
66. Id., p. 109.
67. Leon Friedman, p. 2-5.
68. Blaustein and Zangrando, p. 376.
69. William C. Berman, *The Politics of Civil Rights in the Truman Administration* (Columbus, Oh.: Ohio State University Press, 1970), p. 127.
70. Id., p. 103.
71. *Cassell v. State of Texas*, 339 U.S. 282, 295 (1950) (Frankfurter, J., concurring).
72. *McLaurin v. Oklahoma State Regents for Higher Education*, 339 U.S. 637, 642 (1950).
73. Id., p. 641-42 (emphasis supplied).
74. Brief for Appellants, p. 16.
75. Id., p. 18.
76. Id.
77. Id., p. 65.
78. *Brown v. Board of Education of Topeka*, 347 U.S. 483, 493 (1954).
79. Martin Luther King, Jr., *Stride Toward Freedom*, excerpted in Leon Friedman, p. 34.
80. Taylor Branch, "Uneasy Holiday," *The New Republic* (Feb. 3, 1986), p. 27.
81. Martin Luther King, Jr., "Letter from a Birmingham Jail," in Mortimer J. Adler, ed., *The Negro in American History*, vol. I (Chicago: Encyclopedia Britannica Educational Corp., 1969), p. 195.
82. *The Autobiography of Malcolm X*, excerpted in Leon Friedman, p. 114 (emphasis supplied).
83. Stokely Carmichael, "Power and Racism," in Leon Friedman, p. 142.
84. Id., p. 147.
85. Roy Wilkins, "Whither 'Black Power'?" in Adler, p. 113.
86. Leonard A. Cole, *Blacks in Power* (Princeton, N.J.: Princeton University Press, 1976), p. 99.

87. Id.
88. King, "I Have a Dream," p. 111-12.
89. King, *Where Do We Go From Here*, p. 70.
90. King, "I Have a Dream," p. 112.
91. James Farmer, "Freedom—When?" in Leon Friedman, p. 125.
92. Id., p. 129 (emphasis deleted).
93. Id.
94. Eastland and Bennett, p. 113.
95. *Loving v. Virginia*, 388 U.S. 1, 10 (1967).
96. Abram, p. 1326.
97. Eastland and Bennett, p. 206.
98. Id., p. 207.
99. *Legislative History of Titles VII and XI of the Civil Rights Act of 1964* (Washington, D.C.: United States Equal Employment Opportunity Commission, undated), p. 3015.
100. Abram, p. 1322.
101. *Legislative History*, p. 3187 (remarks of Senator Allott).
102. Simon Rottenberg, ed., *The Economics of Legal Minimum Wages* (Washington, D.C.: American Enterprise Institute for Public Policy Research), p. 5.
103. Bayard Rustin, *Down the Line* (Chicago: Quadrangle Books, 1971), p. 111.

4

The Quest Abandoned

Just as the great civil rights triumphs of the past were followed by crises of victory, so too was the triumph of opportunity in 1964. But while the past crises were resolved by careful reflection and spirited debate culminating in a renewed commitment to the principles of civil rights, the present crisis, now in its third decade, threatens to negate the gains secured through two centuries of struggle and to destroy the nation's dedication to civil rights.

At the very zenith of its achievements, the civil rights movement began to evolve from a "movement" to an "establishment." This metamorphosis was generally not recognized, and it was certainly unheralded, for many of the movement's leaders continued to clothe themselves in the mantle of civil rights. But in reality, for the first time since its genesis, the quest for civil rights was largely abandoned.

The potential for betraying the cause of civil rights is omnipresent, as it is in any political movement, for the lure of power as an end in itself provides a mighty temptation. But in the past, the most successful civil rights leaders consistently resisted the temptation to abuse political power by recognizing that such abuses are antithetical to the cause they championed.

This exercise of self-restraint, however, came abruptly to an end during the 1960s. The reigning leadership began to methodically abandon the traditional goals of the civil rights movement and to dispose of the movement's scrupulous resistance to government coercion, setting out a strategy wholly dependent upon the accretion and exercise of political power. Bayard Rustin personified this sudden departure from established principles, dismissing the "strong moralistic strain in the civil rights movement which reminds us that power corrupts" by declaring "this is not the view I want to debate here, for it is waning."[1]

Ordinarily, an outright reversal of a movement's goals and strategies and a repudiation of its undergirding principles rarely occurs overnight. But the betrayal of civil rights was swiftly effectuated, made possible by a unique combination of forces and events that provided both the impetus and philosophical rationale for this dramatic transformation.

The first factor was the overall social mileau of the 1960s. Despite the vindication of the traditional principles of civil rights marked by the triumph of opportunity, America was in no mood to celebrate. The nation was engulfed in a debilitating convulsion of cynicism and despair, reflected by the escalating war in Vietnam and by the assassinations of John and Robert Kennedy and Martin Luther King. For the first time, America was seriously questioning its fundamental ideals, the very ideals that formed the foundation of the civil rights vision.

The second great influence was the disillusionment among many blacks following the triumph of opportunity. They had been promised "equality"—a term whose meaning had become increasingly confused during the ascendancy of the welfare state. Throughout American history, the meaning of equality had been fairly clear—it referred to equality of opportunity. And at least until the Depression, equality of opportunity almost invariably produced relatively quick results. But as Charles Murray observes, during this period blacks discovered that "equality of rights under the law had not been accompanied by equality of outcome."[2]

The effect of this realization upon blacks was magnified by the depth of past deprivations. Most ethnic minorities had been greeted by basic opportunities upon arrival in America, and generally required only three generations to climb out of poverty.[3] But for blacks, the history of slavery and Jim Crow had delayed opportunity for centuries; in practical terms, the triumph of opportunity secured for blacks only the same prospects that traditionally had greeted new immigrants. Having finally attained that opportunity, many blacks were not content to wait another three generations to escape their impoverished condition.

Indeed, unlike most immigrants who had encountered discrimination but who enjoyed opportunity from the outset, the basic American ideals had lost some of their lustre for blacks through two centuries of deprivations. Historian Winthrop Jordan postulates that if the black man had been liberated at the time of the Revolution rather than a century later, "[t]he implications of the natural rights philosophy . . . would have operated directly upon his nature unimpeded by his glaring status as a slave."[4] Thus, many blacks may have perceived far less of a vested interest in traditional civil rights principles, particularly in the short-run, than did other ethnic minorities who never had to deal with a color line. Consequently, many blacks were receptive to an ideology that would translate equality of opportunity into equality in outcome, shortcutting the integral steps in between.

A third influential factor was the challenge of the black separatists, who exploited the identity crisis that wracked the nation during this period. Although the separatists embraced the very race-consciousness that blacks had endeavored to overcome for generations, theirs was the only prominent program that preserved some measure of self-esteem for blacks by advocating group pride, self-help, and independence, thereby providing an attractive alternative to the paternalistic welfare state. In contrast to the essentially structural objectives of the traditional civil rights movement, the separatists offered tangible and immediate, if dubious, rewards. In order to resist this challenge and preserve its leadership role, the "mainstream" movement felt impelled to offer materialistic incentives as well.

As a consequence, many of those who had come to be identified as the civil rights leadership crafted a revised agenda, incorporating many of the collectivist tenets advocated by the separatists. Bayard Rustin explained the "civil rights movement is evolving from a protest movement into a full-fledged *social movement*—an evolution calling its very name into question."[5] In an effort to preserve their moral legitimacy, these revisionists nonetheless retained the mantle of "civil rights" they had earned in previous decades. In this way, observes Nathan Glazer, the revisionists enjoy an "enormous advantage. They are seen as moral, and a moral advantage in politics, being on the side of right, is worth a good deal."[6]

But the revisionists purveyed a civil rights agenda in name only. The shift in focus was deceptively subtle, relying upon familiar terms with broad support such as "freedom" and "equality." In reality, however, the revisionists embarked upon an ambitious new program of social engineering and wealth redistribution that is profoundly antithetical to the traditional civil rights vision. Their strategy was equally deviant, embracing the very techniques that civil rights advocates had rejected for two centuries. As Bayard Rustin glibly revealed, "How are these radical objectives to be achieved? The answer is simple, deceptively so—*through political power*."[7] For the first time, those invoking the mantle of civil rights would use the power of the state to invade the fundamental rights of others.

Just as the Southern supremacists had searched for a theoretical justification for their drastic departure from the principles of civil rights a century earlier, the contemporary revisionists required a rationale for their agenda. The key to this process was the redefinition of the term "equality." As Charles Murray observes, until 1964,

> most whites (and most blacks) thought in terms of equal access to opportunity. Blacks who failed to take advantage were in the same boat as whites who failed to take advantage. By 1967 this was not an intellectually acceptable way to conceive the issue.[8]

Sociologist Anne Wortham summarizes the ideological premises of the revised agenda as "the priority of equality over freedom and individual rights, the redefinition of equality of opportunity to mean equality of condition or result, the practice of sacrificing principles to pragmatic expediency, and the reliance on government to force into existence solutions to social problems."⁹

This transformation was legitimized by a group of theorists who provided the philosophical underpinnings of the revised agenda. Foremost among them was Michael Harrington, whose *The Other America* in 1963 provided a justification for the redefinition of "equality" to mean outcome rather than opportunity. Harrington depicted "an affluent society," enjoying the "highest standard of life the world has ever known," within whose midst exists in stark contrast "an under-developed nation, a culture of poverty," which is "beyond history, beyond progress, sunk in a paralyzing, maiming routine."¹⁰ For Harrington, the triumph of opportunity was illusory. The poor, he asserted, "are so submerged in their poverty that one cannot begin to think about free choice. . . . [S]ociety must help them before they can help themselves."¹¹ Individual opportunity in such instances, Harrington contended, was meaningless; "[t]here is only one institution in society capable of acting to abolish poverty. That is the Federal Government."¹²

Echoing Harrington's analysis was Christopher Jencks, who eschewed traditional mechanisms for upward social advancement such as education, in favor of government paternalism. Jencks proclaimed that "[w]e need to establish the idea that the federal government is responsible not only for the total amount of the national income, but also for its distribution."¹³ Jencks thus absolved blacks of any responsibility for improving their condition, marking a major shift in approach portending important and disastrous consequences for blacks.

To effectuate this ambitious equality in outcome—without relying on the market mechanisms that the revisionists disdained—would require, of course, massive government coercion, similar to the market-distorting techniques of the Jim Crow era, but with a primary emphasis on income redistribution and a different set of beneficiaries. But such coercion to benefit a minority would necessarily require the sanction of a sizable portion of the majority. It is one thing—and difficult enough—to convince a majority to support equal rights; it is yet another to convince it to volitionally subordinate its own rights in favor of the minority.

The rationale advanced for such a subordination was guilt—white Americans were adjudged guilty of imposing the condition of slavery, and were held responsible for its manifestations, which were viewed to encompass every conceivable malady afflicting blacks. In order to redeem itself, the majority was called upon not only to ensure freedom and opportunity for blacks, but to furnish "reparations" as well. Author Charles Silberman argued for such reparations in 1962 when he declared that the problems of blacks are the result of "sins for which all Americans are in some measure guilty and for which all Americans owe some act of atonement."[14] As Morris Abram observes, this rationale is premised upon a "simplistic division of our complex society into white males and their victims."[15]

This assigned guilt was understandably greeted with derision among many non-blacks, vast numbers of whom were themselves ethnic minorities or descendents of immigrants who overcame prejudice and other barriers not by asking special favors, but by exploiting the equality of opportunity that was the hallmark of the American Dream. But the Johnson administration, attempting to maintain its "liberal" reputation and perhaps seeking to salve its own guilt over the escalating war in Vietnam, embraced the reparations mentality as the cornerstone of its "Great Society" program. President Johnson signalled the premature end of the golden decade of civil rights—and the beginning of a tragic new era—in his commencement speech at Howard University in 1965, declaring that "[w]e seek not just . . . equality as a right and a theory but equality as a fact and equality as a result."[16]

To achieve their ends, the revisionists adopted strategies tailored to the new definition of equality. The head-spinning swiftness with which the former champions of color-blindness embraced color-consciousness once someone else's ox was being gored would have been comic were it not so tragic. Nathan Glazer noted the irony underlying this shift in tactics:

> In 1964, we declared that no account should be taken of race, color, national origin, or religion in the spheres of voting, jobs, and education. . . . Yet no sooner had we made this national assertion than we entered into an unexampled recording of the records of the color, race, and national origin in every significant sphere of [a person's] life. Having placed into law the dissenting opinion of *Plessy v. Ferguson* that our Constitution is color-blind, we entered into a period of color and group-consciousness with a vengeance.[17]

In essence, as Morris Abram observes, the movement "turned away from its original principled campaign for equal justice under law to engage in an open contest for social and economic benefits conferred on the basis of race."[18]

The revisionists introduced three key concepts that would provide the foundation for the legal and public policy innovations necessary to further their objectives. The first concept was one that had been explicitly rejected by every civil rights advocate—and in every civil rights law—since the nation's founding: the notion that rights in *groups*, apart from the individuals that constitute those groups. The revisionists reasoned that since slavery and subsequent forms of racist deprivations were based on race, government policies designed to overcome the effects of such deprivations should similarly be predicated on race. Bayard Rustin identified this concept as the feature that distinguished the contemporary movement from its "classical" antecedents—the "victory of the concept of collective struggle over individual achievement as the road to Negro freedom."[19] The immutable characteristic of race, which was once deemed an inherently irrelevant, invidious factor upon which distinctions must *never* be drawn, was suddenly reinvigorated into an acceptable—indeed *dispositive*—basis for dispensing burdens and benefits in myriad contexts. Thus, like the founding fathers who proclaimed the rights of man while condoning slavery, the revisionists condemned racism while embracing race-consciousness. In so doing, they sacrificed their own past principles and even re-wrote history. Thus, Mary Frances Berry and Blandina Cardenas Ramirez, two members of the U.S. Civil Rights Commission, would somehow claim that "[c]ivil rights laws were not passed to give civil rights protection to all Americans,"[20] while Benjamin Hooks, executive director of the NAACP, would nullify the greatest achievement of the civil rights movement by asserting that "[t]he Constitution was never color-blind."[21] In the process, many of the achievements won through painstaking efforts in the past were abandoned in return for dubious material rewards and political power.

Building upon the definition of equality as contemplating equal outcomes, the revisionists also altered the meaning of "discrimination." Discounting the truism that volitional individual choices can lead to different results among groups, the revisionists perceived only two possible explanations for disparities in outcomes—innate inferiority or discrimination. Since they rejected the former, they adduced that discrimination must account for all differences in outcomes among groups.[22] As Professor Glenn Loury explains,

> [I]n the 1960s a very powerful idea was born, the widespread acceptance of which has made it very difficult for advocates of blacks' interests to acknowledge any diminution in discrimination. This idea . . . is the general presumption that, due to our history of social oppression, blacks' failure to reach parity in American society derives exclusively from the effects of past and ongoing racism, and can only be remedied through state intervention.[23]

The notion that all black problems can be attributed to racism, Loury concludes, "serves to rationalize the embarassing pathology of the ghetto, even as it legitimizes transfers to the black middle class."[24]

Moreover, by defining discrimination in terms of disparities and outcomes, it can be discerned by reference to statistics. "Equality can be measured," proclaimed Jesse Jackson. "It can be turned into numbers."[25]

As Whitney Young argued, this definition offers far more concrete results than "the superficial 'equality of opportunity' that gets so much lip service. ... The measure of equality has to be group achievement: when, in each group in our society, roughly the same proportion of people succeed and fail, then we will have true equality."[26]

The critical flaw in this approach, as Dr. Walter Williams observes, is that "[n]umbers-based civil rights policy ignores individual differences in preferences, ambitions and ability." But, he adds, it is extremely useful to the revisionists because "[s]uch a theory forms an *a priori* basis for establishing the 'right' percentage of blacks in occupations, income groups or in jail, but for the fact of racial discrimination."[27] By defining discrimination in terms of group "underrepresentation," the revisionists removed the critical "intent" element from the offense of discrimination, while providing a justification for "remedies" tailored not to actual victims of discrimination but to the presumptively aggrieved group.

The final key element of the revisionists' strategy was the transformation of welfare and reparations into "rights" due for past deprivations. Thus could Whitney Young demand such niceties as "family allowances ... *as a matter of right*,"[28] guaranteed minimum incomes as a "*right* to which people are entitled,"[29] and "every family's *right* to a decent home."[30] By deriving these rights from the concept of reparations, the revisionists avoided the necessity of justifying the invasion of other people's basic rights that the fulfillment of these newly created "rights" would necessitate.

One could have predicted, of course, that the cycle of poverty depicted by Michael Harrington would *worsen* rather than improve when welfare became a right rather than a form of charity, or when jobs were allocated not according to merit or skill but by proportional representation; and indeed, subsequent events demonstrate that such a dire prediction would be painfully borne out. But such was the racial spoils system embraced by the revisionists; and to question it as counter-productive and harmful to its purported beneficiaries, or to attack it as a nullification of the principles of civil rights, was to be branded a reactionary and a pariah. Few were willing to challenge the assumptions of the civil rights establishment, and those who did so lacked credibility due to the moral monopoly enjoyed by the revisionists.

Indeed, far from the spirit of individualism and free thought that traditionally typified the civil rights movement, the revisionists adopted an authoritarian approach that stifled dissension and debate. Michael Harrington counseled that the poor "will achieve the protection of the welfare state when there is a movement in this land so dynamic and irresistable that it need not make concessions."[31] The revisionist leaders sought to fulfill this prescription, and imposed a stifling intellectual orthodoxy geared to their basic premises. Morris Abram charges that the revisionists effectively ousted many of the "moderate Americans, both black and white, who sustained the movement from the start." The leadership, he recounts, "made support for the redistribution of . . . rights a precondition for being part of the movement; anyone who does not support this redistribution is labelled a racist."[32] As if to prove Abram's point, John E. Jacob, president of the National Urban League, recently illustrated both the movement's authoritarian orthodoxy as well as its wholesale departure from the ideal of equal opportunity in stating that

> [t]he goal of parity between the races is the one constant that must be shared by anyone who presumes to hold a leadership position in the black community. And that goal refers not simply to equality before the law, but equality in all aspects of life. For black inequality is far more blatantly seen disproportionate poverty than in the relatively smaller disparities in the enjoyment of constitutional rights.[33]

The revisionists marshalled their core concepts to engineer a fundamental redistribution of wealth and to mount a comprehensive assault against the principles of individual rights and equal opportunity in courtrooms and legislatures throughout the land. These concepts quickly manifested themselves in every aspect of inter-personal commerce, profoundly altering not only the relationship between the individual and the state, but permeating as well volitional relationships among individuals wholly apart from the context of discrimination.

Nowhere were the ramifications of this new strategy more divisive and disastrous than in the area of public education. The promise of *Brown* was a cause for tremendous optimism for minority children—for the first time, they were entitled to the same opportunities as white children. And for several years following the *Brown* decision, courts continued to sweep aside arbitrary discriminatory barriers that had been erected by state and local governments.

But along with the revised agenda came a movement away from desegregation toward proportional representation as an end in itself. The goals of equal opportunity and freedom of choice were supplanted by an obsession with forced equality of outcome—measured not in terms of educational attainment but of numerical parity between the races. Thus, *Brown* was turned on its head: a decision that demanded no distinctions be drawn on the basis of schoolchildren's skin color was abandoned in favor of pupil assignments made solely on the basis of race; a decision that stressed educational opportunity for all children on an equal basis was negated in favor of race balancing. The mechanism selected to achieve these ends was forced busing, in whose wake lies the accumulated carnage of wrecked public school systems and the shattered dreams of thousands of mis-educated children of all races.

The courts ushered this movement along in incremental fashion, moving farther afield from the mandate of the Fourteenth Amendment and the Civil Rights Act with each decision. In *Green v. County School Board of New Kent County*, the Supreme Court repudiated the notion of free choice in public education, striking down a plan in which a large majority of blacks voluntarily opted to attend a previously segregated school. Speaking for the Court, Justice Brennan remarked that "all that we decide today is that . . . 'freedom of choice' is not an end in itself."[34] In *Swann v. Charlotte-Mecklenburg Board of Education*, the Supreme Court upheld a judicial decree ordering race-based teacher reassignments, racial ratios in student assignments, altered attendance zones, and busing. The Court refused to disturb the district court's conclusion that "in order to live in a pluralistic society each school should have a prescribed ratio of Negro to white students reflecting the proportion for the district as a whole."[35] And in *Keyes v. School District No. 1*, court-ordered busing in Denver was sustained even though students had never been assigned to schools on the basis of race.[36] Thus, courts were empowered to inflict drastic social dislocation wherever they found schools in which students of one race or another were significantly "underrepresented"—even if legal barriers to integration had never existed.

The Supreme Court eventually marked the outer boundaries of this doctrine, decreeing by a slim 5-4 majority in *Milliken v. Bradley* in 1974 that busing could not exceed school district boundaries in most circumstances.[37] And in *Spangler v. Pasadena City Board of Education*,[38] the Court, over a dissent by Justices Brennan and Marshall, held that lower courts could not continually readjust attendance zones where there was no evidence that the school district was responsible for segregation. But although *Milliken* and *Spangler* provided a welcome respite, they did little to resuscitate the principle of equal opportunity as the focus of civil rights laws.

Accordingly, school districts in which discriminatory barriers have long since been eradicated remain shackled by the federal judiciary. The Denver school system, for instance, remains hostage to the federal district court, which has controlled virtually every facet of its functions for nearly two decades—despite the fact that the district was never found guilty of intentional discrimination, and even though some of the original plaintiffs have petitioned the court to lift its control. The Denver plaintiffs' petition to liberate their schools from judicial control reflects a growing concern among black parents, as described by columnist William Raspberry, that court-imposed busing "is almost monomaniacally concerned with the maximum feasible mixing of races, with educational concerns a distant second."[39]

The revisionists' obsession with proportional representation in the public schools has produced debilitating consequences for those in whose name the strategy is invoked. First and foremost, it implies the very stigma of inferiority that *Brown* attempted to eradicate when it rejected the concept of "separate but equal." Central to the "proportional representation" concept is the presumption that free choice is not enough—blacks can progress *only* if they are balanced with whites. As U.S. Civil Rights Commission Chairman Clarence Pendleton has remarked, it as almost as if something "magical happens to black or white kids because they sit down beside one another in the classroom."[40]

But tragically, the only magic in busing is a disappearing act on the part of white students and educational opportunities.[41] White parents, many of whom have no objection to integrated schools,* remove their children from the public system or move out of the community altogether when faced with the prospect of forced busing and the diversion of educational resources to engage in social engineering. The goal of proportional representation thus invariably becomes—as in the case of Denver—a never-ending, self-defeating enterprise. Where the revisionists have succeeded in moving beyond the eradication of barriers to opportunity and substituting race balancing for freedom of choice, they have set into motion a perpetual, vicious cycle of doom and despair: the school district diverts scarce resources into social engineering at the expense of educational quality; individuals who can afford to do so leave, resulting in further racial imbalance; resulting in more judicial intervention; resulting in more efforts to attain numerical parity; resulting in yet additional defections. The cycle repeats itself *ad infinitum*, until educational opportunity is extinguished for everyone. In a perverse sense, the revisionists can at this point in the process be said to have attained their elusive equality in result, for everyone is equally ravaged. Nathan Glazer notes the irony of this particularly tragic manifestation of the revised agenda:

---

*The proof of this contention lies in the fact that many white parents who engage in "flight" from the public schools end up volitionally sending their children to well-integrated private schools. The choice, then, is typically not between integration and segregation, but between the quality education provided by private schools as opposed to the social engineering and hassles of busing in the public system. Judging by the large and growing numbers of minority children in urban private schools, it appears that there is significant "minority flight" from the public schools as well. For a more detailed discussion of this phenomenon, see Chapter 6.

Constitutional law often moves along strange and circuitous paths, but perhaps the strangest yet has been the one whereby, beginning with an effort to expand freedom—no black child shall be excluded from any public school because of his race—the law has ended up with as drastic a restriction of freedom as we have seen in this country in recent years: No child, of any race or group, may 'escape' or 'flee' the school to which that child has been assigned on the basis of his or her race.[42]

In tandem with the push for race balancing in the schools has developed a movement toward proportional representation in employment and higher education, also using the legal construct that equates "underrepresentation" with discrimination. In this area, the vehicle selected to achieve the revisionists' objectives is racial preferences. Like busing, racial preferences tacitly validate the racist notion that equal opportunity is not sufficient for black progress. Clarence Thomas, chairman of the Equal Employment Opportunity Commission (EEOC), charges that the underrepresentation construct and the racial preferences that result are premised upon "some inherent inferiority of blacks ... by suggesting that they should not be held to the same standards as other people," even if those standards are race-neutral,[43] thus raising doubts in the public's minds about the legitimate achievements of individual blacks. Even more fundamentally, such preferences undo the great work of the civil rights movement and open the door to a new era of racial discrimination by providing a rationale with which government may once again freely allocate burdens and benefits solely on the basis of race.

This new race-consciousness insinuated itself into public policy in an inauspicious manner. President Johnson issued Executive Order 11246 in 1965, requiring governmental contractors to "take affirmative action to ensure that applicants are employed, and that employees are treated during employment, without regard to their race, color, religion, sex, or national origin." Given the order's clearly expressed nondiscrimination mandate, a plain reading of the term "affirmative action" could only mean race-neutral efforts to guarantee equal opportunity, such as expanded recruitment and training programs, careful review of employment decisions, uniform application of standards, and so on. But the Department of Labor, charged with implementing the order, ignored this plain meaning and plunged into the quagmire of racial preferences. Instead of mandating positive steps to eradicate discrimination, the Department of Labor instructed federal contractors to adopt specific "goals and timetables" to ensure proportional representation.[44] The concept of "affirmative action" was thus transformed into a high-sounding subterfuge for discrimination.

The Supreme Court gave credence the revisionists' underrepresentation construct in *Griggs v. Duke Power Co.* in 1971.[45] In *Griggs*, the Court unanimously invalidated the employer's hiring requirement of a high school diploma or a passing grade on an intelligence examination. The Court instructed that to challenge such an employment criterion, a plaintiff need not show that it was discriminatorily devised or applied, but simply that its impact falls disproportionately upon blacks. The *Griggs* case, however, involved an employer with a history of racial discrimination—a key factor whose existence renders racial disparities in the workforce suspicious, but which subsequent court decisions applying *Griggs* have routinely overlooked.

Subsequent decisions have focused upon the "adverse impact" theory set forth in *Griggs* to allow them to find discrimination even absent proof of intentional discrimination, thereby limiting employer discretion to utilize employment criteria that do not discriminate but which result in "underrepresentation." A conviction record, for instance, may signal a basic lack of trustworthiness that an employer may wish to use to weed out undesirable applicants. If the employer applies that criterion to blacks and whites alike, there is no discrimination in the ordinary sense of the word. But the underrepresentation construct would nonetheless preclude the use of this criterion if more blacks than whites have conviction records. This, in turn, insulates individuals from the consequences of their actions, ensuring they will not be disadvantaged by the fact that they have committed crimes or failed to receive diplomas. The short-run effect may be increased employment for certain groups, but the long-run implications may be disastrous in terms of sending the wrong signals about taking responsibility for the consequences of one's actions.

Moreover, the underrepresentation construct embodied in federal regulations and case law provides incentives to employers to discriminate in favor of minorities in order to attain proportional representation and avoid lawsuits. For if employers decline to adopt preferences "voluntarily," the courts have made it clear they will do it for them in the face of statistical disparities. The Civil Rights Act has thus been transformed from a nondiscrimination statute into a proportional representation law, which "remedies" discrimination by requiring a different kind discrimination.

Indeed, the issue of whether discrimination is permissible if it is designed to achieve proportional representation is one that seemingly could have been easily resolved within the unambiguous color-blind framework of the Fourteenth Amendment and the Civil Rights Act. But in adopting the underrepresentation construct, the courts have sanctioned a serious departure from the clear meaning of those bulwarks of individual rights and equal opportunity. In *Griggs* and its progeny, the courts implied that *groups* have a right to equal outcomes; and that past acts of discrimination can properly be remedied not by making whole the victims of discrimination, but by conferring entitlements upon random group members. Thus, the notion of utilizing group preferences to "cure" underrepresentation—though considered ludicrous by the framers of the Civil Rights Act—has become a focal point in the battle over the revised agenda.

In order to rationalize their demand for preferences, the revisionists were forced to abandon other vital traditional civil rights principles as well. Foremost among these was the principle that racial discrimination is *never* justifiable. Ignoring Thomas Paine's prophetic warning, echoed consistently by every great civil rights advocate, that once departures from that principle were made it would be impossible to stop—and overlooking the lessons of *Dred Scott, Plessy v. Ferguson*, and *Korematsu*, which had borne out Paine's prophesy—the revisionists proceeded to define a certain species of discrimination as "benign." Racial discrimination, they averred, is not an evil in and of itself; it depends upon which group is the beneficiary. Of course, the white supremacists of the Jim Crow era could have made the same argument. Shorn of its rhetorical pretenses, the issue of preferences, as Charles Krauthammer, one of its apologists recently conceded, "has ceased to be rights. It is group advancement."[46] The argument is no longer one of morality, Krauthammer adds, because such preferences are admittedly a "breach of justice."[47] But, posits Krauthammer, while the interest of justice in ensuring color-blindness is "narrow" and "ambiguous," the "rapid integration of blacks into American life is an overriding national goal and . . . affirmative action is the means to that goal."[48] For the advocates of "benign" racism, it seems, the ends justify the means.

This issue first presented itself to the Supreme Court in 1974 in *DeFunis v. Odegaard*, in which Marco DeFunis, a white applicant with superior credentials, was denied admission to the University of Washington law school in favor of less-qualified minorities. When the case reached the Supreme Court, Justice William O. Douglas viewed the racial preferences applied by the state just as any veteran of the civil rights movement should—he considered them invalid on their face. Douglas looked for support to Justice Thurgood Marshall, the former civil rights lawyer who had forcefully proclaimed in his argument in *Brown* twenty years earlier "[t]hat the Constitution is colorblind is our dedicated belief."[49] In a response that tragically symbolized the wholesale abandonment of traditional principles by the former champions of civil rights, Justice Marshall glibly replied to Douglas, "You guys have been practicing discrimination for years. Now it is our turn."[50]

The Court disposed of *DeFunis* without reaching the substantive issues, holding the case was moot since the plaintiff had ultimately been admitted to law school pursuant to a lower court's injunction. But Douglas dissented from the finding of mootness and addressed the fundamental issues at hand. This case, Douglas argued, was no different than any other race discrimination case, since "the school did not choose one set of criteria but two, and then determined which to apply to a given applicant on the basis of his race."[51] Douglas concluded that a school may appropriately look at subjective factors in assessing applicants, such as special burdens that hindered academic development; and he conceded that minorities might be the principal beneficiaries of such an approach. But the "difference between such a policy and the one presented by this case," Douglas explained, "is that the [university] would be making decisions on the basis of individual attributes, rather than according to a preference solely on the basis of race."[52] Douglas expressly repudiated the underrepresentation construct, declaring the state "may not proceed by racial classification to force strict population equivalencies for every group in every occupation, overriding individual preferences. The Equal Protection Clause commands the elimination of racial barriers."[53]

For Justice Douglas, the principle of constitutional color-blindness was an absolute one, regardless of how "benign" or "compelling" the reasons for exceptions. He warned, "If discrimination based on race is constitutionally permissible when those who hold the reins can come up with 'compelling' reasons to justify it, the constitutional guarantees acquire an accordionlike quality."[54] Applying the clear rule of the Fourteenth Amendment to the plight of Marco DeFunis, Douglas concluded,

> A DeFunis who is white is entitled to no advantage by reason of that fact; nor is he subject to any disability, no matter what his race or color. Whatever his race, he had a constitutional right to have his application considered on its individual merits in a racially neutral manner.[55]

Douglas was no longer a member of the Court when it revisited the issue four years later in the *Bakke* case. This time, the Court addressed the substantive issues, but literally split down the middle in doing so. In *Bakke*, the Court reviewed the University of California at Davis medical school admissions program, which set aside sixteen of 100 seats for specified minorities. The case squarely presented the question of whether the state could apportion admissions solely on the basis of race. The California Supreme Court had struck down the quota as a violation of equal protection, and now the U.S. Supreme Court was called upon to determine whether the broad language of the amendment meant what it clearly said. The brief of the Anti-Defamation League captured the essence of the issue at hand: "Since whites and non-whites by definition exhaust the universe, to what are the rights of non-whites to be equal, if not the rights of whites?"[56]

The Court split three ways. Four justices—Marshall, Brennan, White, and Blackmun—believed the quota was lawful. Four others—Stevens, Stewart, Rehnquist, and Chief Justice Burger—did not reach the question of constitutionality because they concluded the quota was illegal under the color-blind mandate of Title VI of the Civil Rights Act of 1964.[57] The deciding vote was cast by Justice Lewis F. Powell, who issued the Court's judgment. Powell ruled, in combination with four justices, that the strict quota was impermissible; but he joined Marshall and his cohorts in ruling that the university could properly take some account of race. But while Powell did not specify the outermost parameters of such permissible governmental race-consciousness, his opinion emphasized that any exceptions to the principle of race neutrality are extremely narrow. Powell's opinion made it clear that the Fourteenth Amendment protects the rights of *all* citizens, declaring the "guarantee of equal protection cannot mean one thing when applied to one individual and something else when applied to a person of another color. If both are not accorded the same treatment, then it is not equal."[58] Flatly rejecting a relaxed standard of review, Powell declared that all state-imposed racial classifications are "inherently suspect and thus call for the most exacting judicial examination."[59]

Powell's subsequent analysis probed and exposed the tenuous philosophical construct within which the quota was advanced. The constitutional revisionism purveyed by the quota's supporters, Powell explained,

> urges us to adopt for the first time a more restrictive view of the Equal Protection Clause and hold that discrimination against members of the white "majority" cannot be suspect if its purpose can be characterized as "benign." The clock of our liberties, however, cannot be turned back to 1868. . . . It is too late to argue that the guarantee of equal protection to *all* persons permits the recognition of special wards entitled to a degree of protection greater than that accorded others.[60]

As had Paine two centuries earlier, Powell submitted that the "concepts of 'majority' and 'minority' necessarily reflect temporary arrangements and political judgments," and thus provide no "principled basis" upon which to apply different constitutional rules.[61] "By hitching the meaning of the Equal Protection Clause to these transitory considerations," Powell observed, judicial scrutiny of state-imposed racial discrimination could "vary with the ebb and flow of political forces."[62] Powell also viewed the quota as potentially harmful to its purported beneficiaries in the long-run, since "preferential programs may only reinforce common stereotypes holding that certain groups are unable to achieve success without special protection based on a factor having no relationship to individual worth."[63]

Having exposed the flaws in the revisionists' construct, Powell emphasized the importance of civil rights as fundamental, *individual* rights held in equal measure by all:

> If it is the individual who is entitled to judicial protection against classifications based upon his racial or ethnic background because such distinctions impinge upon personal rights, rather than the individual only because of his membership in a particular group, then constitutional standards may be applied consistently.[64]

Applying this analysis, Powell easily concluded that the Davis quota was invalid.

Although Powell's analysis is generally consistent with the civil rights vision that animated the Fourteenth Amendment, it has been largely ignored in subsequent jurisprudence dealing with state-imposed racial preferences. Instead, the revisionists have focused upon the dissenting views of Justices Brennan, Marshall, and Blackmun.[65] In setting forth these views, Justice Brennan summarily dispensed with the vision that had driven the civil rights movement from its genesis through its resonant articulation at the Lincoln Memorial by Martin Luther King, substituting in its place what would become the shibboleth of the revisionists. Rejecting any "static definition of discrimination,"[66] Brennan reminded his colleagues that "no decision of this Court has ever adopted the proposition that the Constitution must be colorblind."[67] Brennan contended that "no fundamental right is involved here" since "whites as a class" have not been victimized by discrimination in the past.[68] Racial preferences, Brennan concluded, are valid "where there is a sound basis for concluding that minority underrepresentation is substantial and chronic."[69] Similarly, Justice Marshall, in his separate opinion, once again illustrated the revisionist history necessary to sanction race-consciousness, declaring that the rule of color-blindness he once advocated would substitute "abstract equality for the genuine equality the [Fourteenth] Amendment was intended to achieve."[70] But it was Justice Blackmun who best captured the frightening illogic of the dissenters' approach, asserting that "[i]n order to get beyond racism, we must first take account of race. . . . And in order to treat some persons equally, we must treat them differently."[71] Thus did the dissenters craft a rationale by which the guarantee of equal protection of the laws could be effectively purged from the Constitution.

Nonetheless, because the dissenters did not prevail, the revisionists viewed the bottom line in *Bakke* with disdain. Congressman Ron Dellums called it "a racist decision," while Jesse Jackson termed it a "devastating blow to our civil-rights struggle" and called for "massive street demonstrations."[72] But their discomfort would be short-lived. The sharply divided

Supreme Court would refuse to squarely address the issues again for eight years, during which time the lower courts were free to march to their own tune and ignore the constitutional principles enunciated by Justice Powell in *Bakke.*

All of the federal courts of appeals have engaged in such frolics, but none so brazenly as the Sixth Circuit in Cincinnati. With the Supreme Court unwilling to constrain it, the Sixth Circuit took the lead in applying the revised agenda. It set out the revised equal protection analysis, which the other circuits would emulate, in *Bratton v. City of Detroit* in 1983. The case involved the city of Detroit, which invented a new form of "separate but equal"—separate promotion lists for blacks and non-blacks in the police department, with half of all promotions accorded to blacks and the other half to non-blacks. Consequently, dozens of non-black sergeants with greater qualifications and seniority were bypassed in favor of blacks who moved ahead of them solely by virtue of their skin color. The city defended the plan as a remedy for past discrimination, but two facts ignored by the court revealed the quota as a naked racial spoils system: the quota was imposed by a black *majority* led by Mayor Coleman Young that controlled all of the city's political machinery, at the expense of whites and other minorities; and most of the quota's beneficiaries were too young to have been victimized by the police department's racial policies many years earlier. Thurgood Marshall's promise of retribution was being carried out by Coleman Young.

In the Sixth Circuit's *Bratton* decision, Judge Nathaniel R. Jones rejected Justice Powell's analysis in *Bakke*, contending "the Brennan-White-Marshall-Blackmun opinion in *Bakke* offer[s] the most reasonable guidance."[73] Applying this rationale, Jones jettisoned both the language and history of the Fourteenth Amendment in ruling that "[o]ne analysis is required when those for whose benefit the Constitution was amended . . . claim discrimination. A different analysis must be made when the claimants are not members of a class historically subjected to discrimination."[74] Jones then exhumed the "reasonableness" test on which infamous *Plessy v. Ferguson* decision was based, with the same results—a victory for "separate but equal." Jones found the quota a reasonable remedy for black "underrepresentation,"[75] a finding based solely upon the fact that the city was 50% black, and which in turn was used to support the conclusion that the police department and its leadership should be 50% black.[76] Through *Bratton* and similar cases, the concept of forced equality in result was now firmly established in American jurisprudence.

The tragic and absurd consequences logically flowing from this approach were perhaps most sympathetically illustrated by the case of Stuart Marsh, a high school guidance counselor in Flint, Michigan. Marsh was hired by the Flint school district as a teacher in 1965, and was promoted to guidance counselor in 1969. Marsh consistently received superb evaluations from both white and black supervisors; but in 1980, shortly before he was eligible to retire, Marsh was demoted from his counselor position in favor of less-senior black counselors pursuant to a racial quota contained in a collective bargaining agreement between the school district and the teachers' union. The Flint school district was never shown to have discriminated; thus the quota was not "remedial" in any sense. Rather, the quota was adopted in order to provide "role models" and cure "underrepresentation." The burden of such social engineering would be borne by Stuart Marsh.

It was no small irony that Stuart Marsh was demoted exactly twenty-five years after Rosa Parks was required to surrender her seat on a public bus in Birmingham. Rosa Parks and Stuart Marsh committed no crimes, but were victimized by the state for exactly the same reasons—they were the wrong color in the wrong place at the wrong time. Mrs. Parks was compelled to step to the back of the bus solely because she was black. Stuart Marsh was forced to step back in his professional standing solely because he was white. Rosa Parks and Stuart Marsh are two sides of the same coin; symbols of the perversity of distinctions in rights predicated upon race.

Marsh filed a claim of race discrimination under the Fourteenth Amendment in federal court for the eastern district of Michigan, which is located in and subordinate to the Sixth Circuit. The case was heard by Judge Stewart Newblatt, a liberal with impeccable civil rights credentials. But Newblatt is one of a handful of liberals in the tradition of William O. Douglas, who had espoused the principles of civil rights in the 1950s and 1960s and who remains faithful to those principles in the 1980s. Judge Newblatt's opinion, while denying relief to Stuart Marsh under the controlling *Bratton* precedent, stands as perhaps the most resounding indictment of the revised agenda ever issued. Newblatt succinctly set out the issue he faced:

> The case presently before this Court is a civil rights action. Stuart Marsh— the plaintiff—is a white man. But the Constitution and the civil rights laws seem to guarantee that color is not relevant and that government cannot confer benefits nor visit burdens on account of race. Stuart Marsh now asks the Court to make good on this guarantee.[77]

Newblatt then proceeded to apply *Bratton*, and its philosophical antecedents, the dissenting opinions in *Bakke*. Under the "underrepresentation" construct set out in those opinions, Newblatt observed that "virtually *every* industry and activity in both the public and private sectors" could be found guilty of discrimination, thus justifying a race-based "remedy."[78] Since black counselors in Flint were statistically underrepresented in relation to black students, Newblatt concluded that a quota was appropriate under *Bratton* provided it was "reasonable."[79] Newblatt raised doubts about whether *any* state-imposed racial preference could be "reasonable" under the ordinary definition of the term, but he wryly noted that in this area of the law, ordinary definitions were twisted and tortured. Referring to Justice Blackmun's contention in *Bakke* that in order to get beyond racism we must take race into account and that to treat some persons equally we must first treat them differently,[80] Judge Newblatt sardonically observed that "Orwell would have found grist for his mill."[81] Newblatt noted that time and again, history had dramatically demonstrated the disastrous ramifications inherent in such logic:

> The ominous thunder of white hooded night riders, the thick Jim Crow statute books, the horrors of Buchenwald, the concentration camps for Japanese-Americans . . . all of this comes to mind with the subject of governments that have enacted laws predicated on race.[82]

But despite his own profound "misgivings and doubts," Judge Newblatt granted judgment for the school district:

> The constitution, it is sad to say, did utterly nothing for Stuart Marsh. For this Court was bound by its constitutional oath of office to apply—rather than make—the law of the land. This compelled the Court to place its imprimatur on an explicit act of racial discrimination visited on an American citizen.[83]

Judge Newblatt concluded his opinion with the admonition that "American history is a thunderous pronouncement that race conciousness must end."[84] But on appeal, the Sixth Circuit turned a deaf ear to the thunder, affirming Newblatt's sarcasm-laced decision and rejecting Marsh's plea to return to the traditional civil rights principles embodied in the Fourteenth Amendment.

Although the *Marsh* case presented perhaps the most sympathetic fact pattern with which the Supreme Court could apply the brakes to state-imposed racial preferences, the Court first decided two other cases raising issues similar to those presented in *Marsh*. First, in the *Stotts* case in 1984, the Court overturned a decision of the Sixth Circuit by a 6-3 vote, ruling that under the Civil Rights Act a federal district court could not disturb a consent decree and override a seniority plan to impose a racial quota for employee layoffs. The decision by Justice White—who had joined the Brennan dissent in *Bakke*—focused on the individual nature of the rights provided by the Civil Rights Act. The purpose of the act is to provide "make-whole relief only to those who have been actual victims of discrimination,"[85] White explained, and thus "mere membership in the disadvantaged class is insufficient" to justify a "remedy" for past discrimination.[86]

Two years later, the Court struck down a quota contained in a collective bargaining agreement between a school district and a teachers' union providing for layoffs of white schoolteachers in order to retain less-senior black teachers to preserve racial balance. In *Wygant v. Jackson Board of Education*, Justice Powell once again issued the judgment of the Court, joined by four other justices. In his plurality opinion, Powell expressly repudiated the Sixth Circuit's "reasonableness" standard, which "has no support in the decisions of this Court."[87] Instead, Powell reiterated that strict scrutiny applies to *all* state-imposed racial classifications, under which such classifications are valid only if they serve a "compelling state purpose" and if "the means chosen to accomplish that purpose are narrowly tailored."[88] Noting that societal discrimination is insufficient to constitute a compelling interest, Powell insisted upon "particularized findings of past discrimination," without which "a court could uphold remedies that are ageless in their reach into the past, and timeless in their ability to affect the future."[89] Finally, Powell ruled the layoff quota was "too intrusive," since "layoffs impose the entire burden of achieving racial equality on particular individuals, often resulting in a severe disruption of their lives."[90]

In invalidating the quota, Justice Powell also confronted two justifications frequently invoked to sanction racial preferences. First, Powell rejected the argument that a certain percentage of black teachers was necessary to provide "role models," remarking that if "[c]arried to its logical extreme, the idea that black students are better off with black teachers could lead to the very system the Court rejected in *Brown v. Board of Education*."[91] Further, Powell found irrelevant the fact that the quota had been approved by a majority of union members. Rejecting Justice Marshall's contention in dissent that the dispute was not between individuals but between racial groups for which the burden of layoffs was fairly apportioned by the quota,[92] Powell declared that the Constitution "does not allocate constitutional rights to be distributed like bloc grants within discrete racial groups; and until it does, petitioners' more senior colleagues cannot vote away petitioners' rights."[93]

Shortly thereafter, the Court also reversed the Sixth Circuit's decision in *Marsh* and remanded it in light of the *Wygant* decision.[94] But the Court's progress toward vindicating the principles of civil rights in *Wygant* was short-lived. In two decisions after *Wygant*, the Court approved racial "goals" imposed by lower courts on employers who were guilty of past and ongoing discrimination over remedies less intrusive on the rights of innocent third parties.[95] More alarmingly, the Court abandoned all pretense of limiting race and gender preferences to "remedying" past discrimination in *Johnson v. Transportation Agency*. By a 6-3 vote, the Court upheld under the Civil Rights Act a plan by Santa Clara County, California, to produce a workforce whose racial and gender composition in every job category mirrors the local population. The plan provides that for every position in which blacks or women are "underrepresented," race and gender may be counted as "plus factors" to allow blacks and women who meet minimal qualifications to pass over more qualified applicants; and supervisors are required to explain any failure to do so.

Pursuant to the plan, the county promoted Diane Joyce, a white female, to a road dispatcher position over Paul Johnson, a more qualified white male. The district court struck down the plan, finding that it was not justified since the county had never discriminated and that Johnson had failed to receive the promotion solely because of his sex. The Supreme Court upheld the plan, ruling that under the Civil Rights Act an employer may erect preferences whenever there is a statistical imbalance in job categories traditionally dominated by white males, regardless of whether the employer had ever discriminated. Moreover, the plan may remain in effect until *every* such job category attains race and gender balance. Since women were "egregiously underrepresented" among skilled craft positions—for whatever reason—Justice Brennan ruled preferential treatment lawful.[96]

Justice Scalia dissented, joined by Chief Justice Rehnquist and Justice White. The majority opinion, Scalia declared, "effectively replace[s] the goal of a discrimination-free society with the quite incompatible goal of proportionate representation by race and by sex in the workplace."[97] He noted the decision would please politicians, "to whom it provides the means of quickly accomodating the demands of organized groups to achieve concrete, numerical improvement in the economic status of particular constituencies"; as well as many employers, who are willing to engage in preferences to immunize themselves against discrimination suits by minorities.[98] In words reminiscent of Justice Harlan's dissent in *Plessy* nearly a century ago, Scalia lamented,

> In fact, the only losers in the process are the Johnsons of the country, for whom Title VII has been not merely repealed but actually inverted. The irony is that these individuals—predominantly unknown, unaffluent, unorganized—suffer this fate at the hands of a Court fond of thinking itself the champion of the politically impotent. I dissent.[99]

The *Johnson* decision is a major setback in the quest to eradicate consideration of race in American society. It squarely endorses coerced equality of result over equal opportunity, and group rights over individual liberty, inflicting painful new divisions in a society badly in need of healing. Perhaps most disturbing is its premise that above a certain minimal threshold of competence, gradations in qualifications are insignificant and may properly be supplanted by race or gender considerations. In addition to denigrating the accomplishments of minorities and women who have succeeded without special treatment, it sends to society a disastrous message about merit—that for some, the highest standards of excellence are unnecessary. Without such standards, of course, "progress" will be illusory and fleeting.

Fortunately, *Johnson* did not overrule *Wygant*, which continues to govern racial classifications adopted by public employers or imposed by courts. Moreover, while the Supreme Court in *Johnson* abdicated much of its role in ensuring equality under the law, it seems the battle is being won in the court of public opinion. A poll taken shortly after the decision found a substantial majority of Americans—including women by a 2-1 majority as well as a large percentage of blacks—disagree with the result.[100]

Nonetheless, the opinion painfully illustrates how incremental progress is in the quest for civil rights. It took 58 years of enormous effort to move from *Plessy* to *Brown*; it will take the same perseverance and steadfast commitment to principle to move from *Brown* to the time in which the full potential of the Fourteenth Amendment is finally realized and color-blindness is the undisputed law of the land.

Critical to that effort is the recognition that contemporary racial classifications are but a subset of the same evil that civil rights advocates have battled for centuries. Professor Anne Wortham explains that

> *[d]iscrimination* is practiced on the premise that conclusions reached about an ethno-racial group override the thoughts, actions, and character of the individuals belonging to that group. . . . As a form of discrimination, *reverse racism* is instituted on the premise that their common bio-ethnic heritage makes one individual responsible for the ideas, actions, and character of another; that individuals of one generation must pay for the sins of their ancestors; and that random individuals must pay for the injustices committed by the government.[101]

But to defeat this new racism would be to remove a tumor, while leaving the cancer intact, free to spread anew. Certainly there are many human victims of the new racism—the Wendy Wygants, the Stuart Marshes; the schoolchildren, white and black, who are pawns of social engineering. But the greatest casualty—one that victimizes all of us—is the risk of destroying America's commitment to civil rights. Underlying the revised agenda is a complete abandonment of the civil rights vision and repudiation of its three core principles: fundamental rights, which have been distorted and diluted; equal opportunity, which has been replaced by its antithesis, forced equality in result; and individualism, which has been subordinated to the collective, with the tragic result that, as Nathan Glazer observes, "the ethnic characterizations of individuals [are] primary for their personal fate."[102] The once noble quest for civil rights has, as Morris Abram describes it, "degenerate[d] into a crude political struggle between groups seeking favored status."[103]

Many of those who occupy the leadership of the contemporary civil rights establishment have relinquished their claim to moral leadership in the process of pursuing their revisionist agenda. That agenda, as Professor Wortham charges, is "an evasion of the responsibilities of personal freedom and a rationalization of their fear of increased social and political freedom."[104] As Glazer warns, the revisionists have transformed the common understanding of civil rights "from one in which the main note is the expansion of freedom into one in which the main note is the imposition of restrictions."[105] If the revisionists prevail in distorting the definition of civil rights, the fragile consensus achieved after centuries of division may be lost forever.

The quest for civil rights is thus once again in crisis; this time, a crisis of identity that threatens to render it a curious relic of the past with little contemporary relevance. Just as the abolitionists were not content merely to eradicate slavery, just as the "classical" civil rights movement was not satisfied merely to bury Jim Crow, so must the true proponents of civil rights not content themselves today merely with opposing particular deprivations of civil rights, but must instead push forward until the civil rights vision is renewed and its original undergirding principles are established once and for all.

All Americans have a vested interest in civil rights, but it is nearly impossible to fully appreciate that interest when the meaning of civil rights is so distorted as it is today. Once again, the task of reviving the spirit of civil rights—and more fundamentally, of recapturing the moral high ground — is at hand. America can only fulfill the great destiny prescribed by its founders if it renews the principles of civil rights without equivocation or compromise.

Notes

1. Rustin, p. 118.
2. Charles Murray, *Losing Ground* (New York: Basic Books, Inc., 1984), p. 30.
3. Sowell, *Race and Economics*, p. 149.
4. Jordan, p. 374.
5. Rustin, p. 115 (emphasis supplied).
6. Glazer, p. 210.

7. Rustin, p. 118 (emphasis supplied).
8. Murray, p. 33.
9. Anne Wortham, *The Other Side of Racism* (Columbus, Oh: Ohio State University Press, 1981), p. 302-33.
10. Michael Harrington, *The Other America* (Baltimore, Md: Penguin Books, Inc., 1963), p. 159.
11. Id., p. 162.
12. Id., p. 171.
13. Christopher Jencks, *Inequality* (New York: Basic Books, Inc., 1972), p. 264.
14. Eastland and Bennett, p. 128-29.
15. Abram, p. 1323.
16. Marvin E. Gettleman and David Mermelstein, *The Great Society Reader* (New York: Random House, 1967), p. 254.
17. Glazer, p. 31.
18. Abram, p. 1312.
19. Gettleman and Mermelstein, p. 264.
20. Robert Pear, "Civil Rights Agency Splits in Debate on Narrowing Definition of Equality," *New York Times* (Oct. 14, 1985), p. A17.
21. Benjamin L. Hooks, "The U.S. Constitution Was Never Color-Blind," *New York Times* (Nov. 27, 1985), p. A22.
22. Thomas Sowell, *Civil Rights: Rhetoric or Reality?* (New York: William Morrow and Co., Inc., 1984), p. 21.
23. Glenn C. Loury, "The 'Color Line' Today," *The Public Interest* (Summer 1985), p. 95.
24. Id.
25. Eastland and Bennett, p. 7.
26. Whitney M. Young, Jr., *Beyond Racism* (New York: McGraw-Hill Book Co., 1969), p. 152.
27. Walter E. Williams, *Discrimination and Public Policy* (unpublished manuscript presented to the United States Commission on Civil Rights, Mar. 6, 1985), p. 4. The author expresses his appreciation to Dr. Williams for permission to cite this work and for the assistance and inspiration he has consistently provided.
28. Young, p. 176 (emphasis supplied).
29. Id., p. 179 (emphasis supplied).
30. Id., p. 183 (emphasis supplied).
31. Harrington, p. 172.
32. John E. Jacob, "Black Leadership in a Reactionary Era," *The Urban League Review*, vol. 9, p. 42-43 (Summer 1985).
33. Abram, p. 1325.
34. *Green v. County School Board of New Kent County*, 391 U.S. 430, 440 (1968).
35. *Swann v. Charlotte-Mecklenburg Board of Education*, 402 U.S. 1, 16 (1971).
36. *Keyes v. School District No. 1*, 413 U.S. 189 (1973).
37. *Milliken v. Bradley*, 418 U.S. 717 (1974).
38. *Spangler v. Pasadena City Board of Education*, 427 U.S. 424 (1976).
39. William Raspberry, "The Easy Answer: Busing," *Washington Post* (April 10, 1985), p. A23.
40. Clarence Pendleton, "Education and Minorities," *Journal of Social, Political and Economic Opportunities*, vol. 9, p. 73 (Spring 1984).
41. This tragic consequence may finally be widely apparent. See, e.g., Barbara

Vobegda and Molly Moore, "Wide Impact Seen for Norfolk Ruling," *Washington Post* (February 8, 1986), p. A-ll; and Molly Moore, "End to Norfolk Busing Seen as Chance to Rejuvenate Aging City," *Washington Post* (February 9, 1986), p. D-l.

42. Glazer, p. 109-10.
43. Clarence Thomas, "Equal Employment Opportunity Commission," in *Regulatory Program of the United States Government* (Washington, D.C.: Office of Management and Budget, 1985), p. 524.
44. Glazer, p. 46.
45. *Griggs v. Duke Power Co.*, 401 U.S. 424 (1971).
46. Charles Krauthammer, "A Defense of Quotas," *The New Republic* (Sept. 16 & 23, 1985), p. 11.
47. Id.
48. Id.
49. Brief for Appellants, p. 65.
50. William O. Douglas, *The Court Years 1939-75: The Autobiography of William O. Douglas* (New York: Random House, 1980), p. 149.
51. *DeFunis v. Odegaard*, 416 U.S. 312, 325 (1974) (Douglas, J., dissenting).
52. Id., p. 332.
53. Id., p. 342.
54. Id., p. 343.
55. Id., p. 337.
56. Eastland and Bennett, p. 18.
57. *Regents of the University of California v. Bakke*, 438 U.S. 265, 416 (1978) (Stevens, J., dissenting).
58. Id., p. 289-290 (Opinion of Powell, J.).
59. Id., p. 290.
60. Id., p. 294-95.
61. Id., p. 295-96.
62. Id., p. 298.
63. Id.
64. Id., p. 299.
65. Of note is the fact that Justice White, often counted among the revisionists because he joined Justice Brennan's dissent, also joined that portion of Justice Powell's opinion that sets out the "strict scrutiny" standard of review. His subsequent votes in racial preference cases firmly place him outside the revisionist construct.
66. *Bakke*, p. 339 (Brennan, J., concurring in the judgment in part and dissenting in part).
67. Id., p. 336.
68. Id., p. 357.
69. Id., p. 362.
70. Id., p. 398 (Opinion of Marshall, J.).
71. Id., p. 407 (Opinion of Blackmun, J.).
72. Eastland and Bennett, p. 173.
73. *Bratton v. City of Detroit*, 704 F.2d 878, 885 (6th Cir. 1983).
74. Id., p. 886 (quoting *Detroit Police Officers Association v. Young*, 608 F.2d 671, 697 (6th Cir. 1979)).
75. Id., p. 886.
76. Id., p. 893.

77. *Marsh v. Board of Education of City of Flint*, 581 F. Supp. 614, 616 (E.D. Mich. 1984); *aff'd. mem.* 762 F.2d 1009 (6th Cir. 1985); *rev'd.*, 54 U.S.L.W. 3777 (U.S. May 27, 1986).
78. Id., p. 621 (emphasis supplied).
79. Id., p. 622.
80. See note 71 and accompanying text earlier in this chapter.
81. *Marsh*, p. 623.
82. Id.
83. Id., p. 628.
84. Id.
85. *Firefighters Local Union No. 1784 v. Stotts*, 467 U.S. 561, 580 (1984).
86. Id., p. 579.
87. *Wygant v. Jackson Board of Education*, 54 U.S.L.W. 4479, 4483 (U.S. May 20, 1986) (Opinion of Powell, J.). The author was privileged to represent the plaintiffs in *Wygant*, *Marsh*, and *Bratton* at various stages in the appellate process. The plaintiffs in these cases, Wendy Wygant, Stuart Marsh, Hanson Bratton, and their colleagues—like Dred Scott, Adolph Plessy, and Oliver Brown before them—displayed tremendous personal courage in the cause of civil rights. They are the movement's unsung heroes, the pioneers of the new frontiers of civil rights.
88. *Wygant*, p. 4481.
89. Id., p. 4482.
90. Id., p. 4484.
91. Id., p. 4482.
92. Id., p. 4491 (Marshall, J., dissenting).
93. Id., p. 4483 n.8 (Powell, J.).
94. *Marsh v. Board of Education*, 54 U.S.L.W. 377 (U.S. May 27, 1986).
95. *United States v. Paradise*, 55 U.S.L.W. 4211 (U.S. Feb.25, 1987); and *Local 28 of Sheet Metal Workers International Ass'n. v. EEOC*, 54 U.S.L.W. 4984 (U.S. June 24, 1986).
96. *Johnson v. Transportation Agency*, No. 85-1129, slip op. p. 17 (U.S. March 25, 1987).
97. Id., p. 2 (Scalia, J., dissenting).
98. Id., p. 20-21.
99. Id., p. 21.
100. Susan Manuel, "Women say court erred on hiring," *USA Today* (March 31, 1987), p. 3A.
101. Wortham, p. 29.
102. Glazer, p. 69-70.
103. Abram, p. 1321.
104. Wortham, p. xvii.
105. Glazer, p. 110.

Part II
RECHARTING THE COURSE OF CIVIL RIGHTS

Introduction to Part II

We must return to first principles . . . and think, *as if
we were the* first men that thought.

—Thomas Paine[1]

The preceding Part chronicles the history of the civil rights movement in America, and recounts the methods by which the movement has responded to the crises of victory that have confronted it. The approach during most of America's first two centuries was to resolve crises of victory through a renewed dedication to the civil rights vision, implemented through strategies designed to build upon past successes and overcome remaining obstacles to civil rights. By contrast, the contemporary civil rights establishment, however, has repudiated this approach and turned its back on the traditional principles of civil rights, substituting a revised agenda based on race-consciousness and collectivism.

After more than two decades during which the revised agenda has dominated civil rights policy in America, it is possible to compare the two approaches and determine which has been more successful. Any measure of success, of course, turns on the standards selected. Public policies can be measured both in terms of their consistency with a moral vision, and in terms of practical short-term and long-range consequences. The preceding Part illustrates the moral virtue of the traditional civil rights vision—by guaranteeing equality of individual rights, it comprises the only set of principles incompatible with rule by force. Moreover, the historical retrospective demonstrates that the practical long-term consequences of the traditional approach to civil rights have been extremely positive; whatever its shortfalls, the American experiment has set the standard for civil rights around the world.

The criticisms levelled by the revisionists against the traditional approach are focused, however, on perceived short-term inadequacies. Such criticisms are not surprising considering the principal objectives of the traditional civil rights vision are individual liberty and equal opportunity; advancements in material well-being are a welcome but incidental by-product. Judged in terms of its own priorities, the traditional approach toward civil rights has been quite successful. America's commitment to

81

liberty and opportunity have historically provided the foundation by which generations of newcomers and outsiders have surmounted prejudices, language barriers, and poverty to improve, slowly but surely, their socioeconomic status and secure their share of the American Dream.

For the reasons outlined in the preceding chapter, however, many civil rights leaders in the 1960s altered the movement's traditional priorities and turned instead to the coercive apparatus of the state to produce immediate material progress and socioeconomic parity. Accordingly, the "success" of the revised agenda should be measured not only in terms of the traditional civil rights vision, but also by its own standard of success—significant improvements in material well-being and demonstrable progress toward attaining parity.

Certainly, the revised agenda cannot claim to meet the same high moral standards as the traditional civil rights approach, for it embraces distinctions based on race and color and relies on coercion to accomplish its objectives. Indeed, its proponents rarely resort to moral arguments, focusing instead on socioeconomic advances. But even by this standard, the revised agenda has proven a colossal failure, delivering many of its purported beneficiaries into a new feudalism from which escape may prove impossible.

The revisionists, of course, will object to this assessment, and can certainly trot out numerous "success stories"; but these "successes" have mainly been achieved by the same enterprising individuals who would have succeeded in a competitive marketplace without bearing the stigma of the unearned inherent in the revisionists' paternalistic system—a system that tacitly assumes that blacks and other minorities cannot make it without something more than equal opportunity. In any event, such examples are exceptions to the rule that the revised agenda has ravaged prospects for the material socioeconomic improvement—not to mention the self-esteem— of its purported beneficiaries, while undermining the nation's commitment to the principles that made opportunities available to minorities in the past and enabled them to make tangible progress while preserving their dignity.

As the civil rights establishment itself concedes, income inequalities between whites and blacks have not diminished in the period during which the revised agenda has dominated national civil rights policy. Indeed, the National Urban League reports that the median income of blacks *declined* from 62% of white income in 1960 to 56% in 1984.[2] But amazingly, the Urban League's policy prescription for the future is by and large more of the same statist policies that have throttled black progress during the past two decades!

That the revisionists can continue to advocate their failed agenda underscores the absence of a well-defined alternative based on the traditional civil rights vision. Most of those who oppose the revised agenda have focused almost exclusively upon quotas, busing, and the plight of whites, without producing a positive strategy of their own to address the very real civil rights issues—the denials of individual liberty and equal opportunity—that confront us today. John Bunzel, a former member of the U.S. Commission on Civil Rights, charges that those leading the battle against quotas have failed "to provide a new approach or set of ideas in this area," and that "the debate on civil-rights policy has not been redefined." He assigns the blame to policymakers who arrive at decisions "not by consulting some moral touchstone but by calculating the political costs."[3]

Perhaps in this respect, the revised agenda, like past challenges, is a blessing in disguise in the overall quest for civil rights, because by bringing the issue closer to home, it has opened the eyes of some who were previously indifferent to civil rights. Once again, events have conspired—this time in the form of forced busing, "reverse discrimination," and other deprivations of civil rights—to vividly demonstrate that the only effective defense against threats to civil rights is to unequivocally and absolutely demand those rights for everyone; for it is the exception that devours the rule, time and again. Thus, the cause of civil rights is best served not merely by opposing busing, quotas, and other manifestations of the revised agenda, but by combining that opposition with a positive civil rights strategy. Only then can the civil rights vision be restored and the moral high ground regained. This Part will explore the consequences of the departure from traditional civil rights principles and suggest some alternatives to restore the civil rights movement to its proper course.

Benjamin Hooks, executive director of the NAACP and a principal purveyor of the revised agenda, was correct in his recent assessment of the high stakes at issue: "[T]he struggle before us is, quite literally, for America's soul."[4] That battle will be lost unless the true advocates of civil rights rediscover the creativity, courage, and commitment that are necessary to transform crisis into triumph.

Notes

1. Clark, p. xiv (emphasis supplied).
2. "Improved Economy Is Failing to Reach Most Black Americans, Urban League Says," *Daily Labor Report* (Jan. 24, 1986), p. A-5.
3. John J. Bunzel, "Principle Isn't Likely to Determine Hiring Rules," *Wall Street Journal* (Sept. 9, 1985), p. 24.
4. Hooks, p. A22.

5

The Failed Agenda

Immigrants and members of ethnic minority groups have traditionally warmly embraced the American Creed and the principles of civil rights because they have correctly perceived they had a direct stake in them. Given an equal opportunity and the freedom to succeed or fail, generation after generation improved its socioeconomic condition compared to their predecessors, on the basis of individual merit, ambition, effort, and talent.

When Gunnar Myrdal investigated race relations in the 1940s, he found that blacks shared this commitment:

> Negroes feel that they cannot afford to sell out the rights they have under the Constitution and the American Creed, even when these rights have not materialized and even when there is no immediate prospect of making them a reality. . . . [N]egroes show, by taking this position, that they have not lost their belief than ultimately the American Creed will come out on top.[1]

In the intervening years, of course, two dramatic and contradictory developments occurred that altered the situation that Myrdal reported: first, during the decade spanning 1954-64, America finally extended the basics of the American Creed to blacks by guaranteeing equal opportunity after centuries of deprivation; and second, for the reasons outlined earlier, the civil rights leadership by and large abandoned the traditional principles of civil rights. This metamorphosis—the abandonment of the principles of equal opportunity and individual rights just as they were at the verge of becoming a reality for black Americans—was much akin to building a magnificent skyscraper and thereupon yanking the ground floor out from under it: the inevitable result is the building comes crashing down.[2]

The revised agenda has wrought precisely such a collapse. By almost any measure—and particularly by the standard of material equality in outcome embraced by the revisionists themselves—the revised agenda has utterly failed.

84

Given the impressive strides made by blacks during the Jim Crow era, during which government policy was directed at *restricting* black progress, one might reasonably expect policies designed to *create* equality—such as preferential treatment and massive government spending—would surely produce dramatic progress. Certainly the resources devoted to this objective were not insubstantial; indeed, in terms of social welfare costs alone, spending between 1950-80 increased by 2000%—forty times the growth in population during that period.[3] If equality could possibly be produced in this fashion, remarkable progress should certainly have resulted.

That the revisionists' material objectives were not accomplished is a stark fact of life. But just how miserably the revised agenda failed is revealed in Charles Murray's *Losing Ground*—a work not without its critics,[4] but whose basic conclusions regarding the disastrous effects of the social policy of the past quarter century have infused the contemporary debate over these issues with a painful dose of reality.

Murray found not only that parity has failed to materialize despite tremendous and costly effort, but that earlier progress has been stifled if not reversed. The rate of poverty, for instance, was declining steadily for two decades until 1973, when it turned around and increased along with government welfare spending.[5] With the shift in government policy from encouraging economic independence to ensuring minimum living standards, economic dependency on government—which had decreased by a third between 1950-65—began growing again in the midst of the Great Society's "War on Poverty," with the percentage of Americans depending on social welfare rising from 18.2% in 1968 to 22% in 1980.[6]

Blacks have borne a disproportionate share of recent economic hardships, which is especially tragic since they were making large gains before the reversal in civil rights policy. A recent study by James P. Smith and Finis Welch for the Rand Corporation revealed that in the forty years between 1940-80, blacks rapidly narrowed the socioeconomic gap. During that period, wages of black males increased 52% faster than white wages; in 1940, the typical black male earned only 43% of his white counterpart, but that percentage had grown to 73% by 1980.[7] Gains by black women during this period were even more rapid.[8] Moreover, the black middle class experienced enormous growth, and for the first time it outnumbered the black poor.[9] Similarly, the percentage of black families in poverty decreased substantially, from 75% in 1940 to 30% in 1980.[10]

But strikingly, the study found 80% of black progress between 1940-80 was made *before* 1965[11]—before racial preferences, before massive busing, before skyrocketing welfare spending. Indeed, the decline in the percentage of black families in poverty ceased altogether between 1970-80, at the very height of the welfare state.[12] During the Carter administration, which embraced the revised agenda as its civil rights policy, real incomes of black men actually declined by 5%; whereas since then, they have begun to increase again, growing by 2.3% in the third and fourth years of the Reagan administration, which has emphasized economic growth as the primary mechanism for black progress.[13] Indeed, the study's findings suggest the traditional civil rights approach, despite its emphasis on opportunity rather than outcome, is far more conducive to short-term socioeconomic progress than the revised agenda with its emphasis on compelled equality. Smith and Welch concluded that gains in black income between 1940-70 resulted from increased educational skills and general economic growth,[14] while "affirmative action apparently has [had] no significant long-run effect" on the racial wage gap.[15] In eschewing the traditional mechanisms for upward social advancement that produced such impressive progress between 1940-70, the revisionists have wrought such underwhelming results that if present trends continue, one analyst projects "the median incomes of black and white families in the United States will be equal in about three centuries."[16]

The extent to which black socioeconomic progress has been set back by the revised agenda is difficult to measure; but certainly prospects for a resumption of earlier gains are bleak without a dramatic shift in priorities. In part because of the lure of welfare dependency—and despite racial preferences in employment—the black labor participation rate, which was virtually identical to the rate for whites in 1954, was 8% lower than the white participation rate by 1980.[17] Similarly, in the critical area of education, Murray reports that "as of 1980, the gap in educational achievement between black and white students was so great that it threatened to defeat any other attempts to narrow the economic differences separating blacks and whites."[18] Such is the prognosis for black progress through the revised agenda.

Similar outcomes have resulted for other ethnic groups who have embraced the revised agenda to varying degrees. While incomes for all blacks relative to whites decreased during the height of the revised agenda from 62% in 1969 to 60% in 1977, relative incomes of Mexican-Americans declined from 76% to 73% and of Puerto Ricans from 63% to 50% compared to whites during that same period.[19]

Conversely, ethnic groups that have declined to subscribe to the revised agenda continued to make enormous progress by exploiting the traditional mechanisms provided by the American system. These ethnic groups have not relied on special preferences, yet have overcome such obstacles as prejudice and language barriers; and by utilizing the same methods successfully embraced by scores of earlier immigrants—e.g., entrepreneurial initiative, educational betterment, disdain for welfare—they are well on their way to socioeconomic parity with native-born Americans. A recent survey revealed that foreign-born workers arriving before 1960 had within two decades attained a higher median income ($13,697) than native-born workers ($11,125).[20] Immigrants from Asia in particular have successfully pursued educational and entrepreneurial opportunities, and now surpass native-born earnings with a median income of $12,200.[21] But perhaps most striking is the difference in income between native and foreign-born blacks. Despite language barriers, black immigrants in 1982 enjoyed a median salary of $11,146, nearly as high as native-born whites ($11,512) and far exceeding native-born blacks.[22] Moreover, 29.9% of foreign-born black families have annual incomes of $35,000 or more, compared to only 20.5% of native-born whites and 17% of native-born blacks.[23] Specifically, family incomes of black immigrants from the West Indies are 94% of the national average, and those of their second generation exceed the average.[24] The impressive success of foreign-born blacks suggests the socioeconomic inequality of blacks is not solely attributable to racism, and illustrates the traditional mechanisms for upward mobility are far more effective in reducing inequality than the shortcut methods embraced by the revisionists.

Apart from side-tracking socioeconomic progress, the revised agenda has impacted blacks in yet another deleterious respect—it has widened the gulf between the black middle class and the very poor "underclass." To some extent, this is not coincidental, for as economist Walter Williams observes, more fortunate blacks have justified preferential treatment by invoking the existence of the underclass.[25] Racial preferences increase the demand for highly qualified blacks, who probably would succeed even without them, and have led to steadily increasing incomes for the top fifth of blacks at the same time incomes for the bottom three-fifths have declined. Sine the proliferation of preferences, the average salaries for black male college graduates with significant work experience have increased in relation to their white counterparts to the point of near parity, while salaries for black high school dropouts have declined dramatically in comparison to similarly situated whites.[26] Quotas and "goals" are a cheap and easy substitute for equal opportunity, and the former are often pursued at the expense of the latter. Thus, racial preferences, in the name of aiding all blacks, seem to be helping only those in the upper ranks, while those at the bottom are even worse off than before—a condition exacerbated by the fact that the civil rights establishment by its preoccupation with preferences has made little effort to preserve or broaden traditional mechanisms for upward mobility. Thus, racial preferences may net a few token vice president slots here and there, but at the cost of possibly consigning blacks as a whole to a permanently inferior socioeconomic status. It is the height of tragic irony that an agenda dedicated to integrating blacks into the American system has instead produced even greater isolation than before.

The consequences of the revised agenda cannot be measured in economic terms alone—and the subtle costs are possibly even more pernicious than the more obvious ones. Professor Glenn Loury argues that racial preferences detract from the quest for black progress by reinforcing the notion that successful blacks are "supplicants of benevolent whites":

> [T]he broad use of race preference to treat all instances of "under-representation" introduces uncertainty into the process by which individuals make inferences about their own abilities. . . . It undermines the ability of people to confidently assert . . . that they are as good as their achievements seem to suggest. It therefore undermines the extent to which the personal success of one group member can become the basis of guiding the behavior of other individuals.[27]

By denigrating the achievements of the best and brightest in this manner, the effects of the revised agenda may ultimately prove counterproductive even for those few it promotes. William Raspberry, in a column entitled "Affirmative Action That Hurts Blacks,"[28] describes the experience of Dayna Matthew, a law student at the University of Virginia who, on the basis of a writing competition, was on her way, along with two classmates, to becoming the first black members of the Law Review. But just before their moment of triumph, the Law Review adopted a special program designed specifically to bring in blacks. Said Ms. Matthew, "Affirmative action was a way to dilute our personal victory. I see this well-intentioned, liberal-white-student affirmative action program as an intrusion."

As Raspberry explains, "The glaring danger of the new plan is that it will cast doubt on the true qualifications of all blacks who make Law Review, no matter how qualified they may in fact be." Thus, he concludes the likely results are "(1) to reduce the value of Law Review, particularly for minorities, and (2) to penalize those minorities who would have made it on their own."

These ramifications are compounded by the fact that by equating preferential treatment and other facets of the revised agenda with civil rights, the revisionists are jeopardizing the national commitment to the traditional principles that could provide greater prospects for black Americans.[29] *The New Republic* recently editorialized, for instance, that Jesse Jackson, the putative "president of black America," uses "the rhetoric of unity to divide." By exploiting such incidents as the Howard Beach attack to bolster support for his collectivist program, Jackson drives a wedge between whites and blacks and alienates his followers from traditional American values. As *The New Republic* charges, "All his talk about 'coalition' notwithstanding, common ground is precisely what Jesse Jackson does not want blacks to have with whites. The politics of polarization, which usually comes raw and ugly, has never been delivered so smoothly."[30]

Despite their resounding failures, the revisionists maintain their vice-grip over what is commonly identified in the public's mind as the civil rights movement. Rather than step aside to make room for new ideas like the abolitionists did following emancipation, the present leadership—with some notable exceptions (see Chapter 8)—continues to promote the same statist agenda while growing ever more authoritarian in its attitude toward dissent.

As National Urban League president John E. Jacob remarks, the movement is "still about the hard job of achieving racial parity."[31] This overriding objective can, of course, be achieved if at all only through the coercive apparatus of the state. Jacob urges that "[b]lack people will never achieve equality without a government that protects our rights and provides the basic income, health, housing and educational guarantees necessary for survival."[32] Indeed, among the Urban League's most recent public policy proposals, at least 16 of 24 envision a vastly enlarged role for government.[33]

The revised agenda's defining characteristic, however, is its commitment to racial preferences, which Jacob calls "the litmus test of civil rights."[34] This view reflects what EEOC Chairman Clarence Thomas refers to as the "new orthodoxy," which "stifles . . . meaningful discussion of the countless problems facing blacks today." The "most amazing irony," Thomas adds, "is that those who claim to have the *progressive* ideas have very regressive ones about individual freedoms."[35] Dissenters like Thomas, who oppose racial preferences but embrace the traditional principles of civil rights, are denounced as racists if they are white, or Uncle Toms if they are black. Indeed, if Frederick Douglass or William Lloyd Garrison were alive today and advocated their individualist, color-blind civil rights philosophies, there is little doubt the revisionists would treat them with the same disdain directed at Civil Rights Commission Chairman Clarence Pendleton, Assistant Attorney General William Bradford Reynolds, or other contemporary defenders of the traditional civil rights vision.

But the only present visible alternative to those who preach that blacks can only succeed as wards of the state is voiced by Muslim leader Louis Farrakhan, who has revived the program of self-sufficiency and racial purity advocated by the black separatists of the 1920s and 1960s. Farrakhan's message is virulently anti-Semitic and lacks any coherent practical strategy; but as Howard University professor Ron Walters observes, Farrakhan "fill[s] a void" by telling blacks they can lift themselves to prosperity on their own.[36] Without some clear alternative, demagogues like Farrakhan will attract adherents among blacks who reject the cynical and pessimistic agenda of the contemporary civil rights establishment.

Yet, despite the near monopolization of the civil rights leadership by advocates of preferences, paternalism, and an ever-expanding welfare state, evidence suggests that many blacks are seriously questioning the basic assumptions of the revised agenda, without embracing the racist alternative personified by Louis Farrakhan. A recent national survey revealed a remarkable divergence between the views of black Americans and those commonly identified as black leaders.* For instance, while 77% of the black leaders favored preferential treatment for blacks in employment and higher education, 77% of all blacks *opposed* such preferences.[37] Similarly, 68% of the leaders supported busing while only 47% of all blacks favored it[38]; and more than twice as many blacks approved of President Reagan's performance than did black leaders (30% - 13%).[39]

As Clarence Thomas observes, this survey illustrates that "notwithstanding protestations to the contrary and pressure to conform to some common black thought, . . . black Americans continue to have their own opinions." This is true despite "an obsession with painting blacks as an unthinking group of automatons," argues Thomas, who laments that "[w]e certainly cannot claim to have progressed much in this century as long as it is insisted that our intellects are controlled entirely by our pigmentation."[40]

The abysmal failure of the revised agenda, combined with strong evidence that the civil rights establishment is out of touch with the grass roots, suggests the time is ripe for a well-defined alternative that can compete with the revisionists' enticements. Blacks and other minorities who face discrimination and barriers to equal opportunity can be forgiven if they doubt the sincerity of those who oppose racial preferences without providing a coherent civil rights strategy of their own. The revisionists are at best misguided and at worst demagogic, but at least they offer a clear agenda. Their primacy as civil rights leaders cannot successfully be challenged without a vision and strategy that will aggressively promote individual liberty and equal opportunity.

Those who undertake this mission will inherit a proud—albeit recently tarnished—legacy. But by building upon past triumphs and tenaciously challenging contemporary civil rights deprivations, the decades ahead can be a time of great progress, a time when long overdue commitments are honored for all Americans.

Notes

1. Myrdal, p. 799.

*The leaders surveyed included 105 representatives of the NAACP, National Urban League, Southern Christian Leadership Conference, Operation PUSH, National Conference of Black Mayors, and Congressional Black Caucus.

2. The author is indebted for the writings of the late Ayn Rand for this analogy, which is applicable to myriad contemporary maladies.
3. Murray, p. 14.
4. See, e.g., Robert Greenstein, "Losing Faith in 'Losing Ground,'" *The New Republic* (March 25, 1985), p. 12-17.
5. Murray, p. 58.
6. Id., p. 64-65.
7. James P. Smith and Finis R. Welch, *Closing the Gap: Forty Years of Economic Progress for Blacks* (Santa Monica, Ca: The Rand Corporation, 1986), p. 18.
8. Id., p. 103.
9. Id., p. 19.
10. Id., p. 103.
11. Id., p. xxviii.
12. Id., p. 103.
13. Id., p. xxvi.
14. Id., p. xxviii.
15. Id., p. 95.
16. Reynolds Farley, *Blacks and Whites: Narrowing the Gap?* (Cambridge, Ma: Harvard University Press, 1984), p. 15.
17. Murray, p. 76.
18. Murray, p. 105.
19. Sowell, *Civil Rights: Rhetoric or Reality?*, p. 51.
20. Ellen Sehgal, "Foreign Born in the U.S. Labor Market," *Daily Labor Report* (Aug. 7, 1985), p. D-4.
21. Id., p. D-5.
22. Id.
23. Id.
24. Sowell, *Civil Rights: Rhetoric or Reality?*, p. 77-79.
25. Williams, *Discrimination and Public Policy*, p. 19.
26. Sowell, *Civil Rights: Rhetoric or Reality?*, p. 52-53.
27. Glenn C. Loury, *Beyond Civil Rights* (unpublished manuscript presented to the National Urban League, July 24, 1985), p. 15.
28. William Raspberry, "Affirmative Action That Hurts Blacks," *Washington Post* (February 23, 1987), p. A11.
29. Glazer, p. 69-70.
30. "On the Beach," *The New Republic* (February 23, 1987), p. 8
31. John E. Jacob, "A Movement That Has Made a Difference," *Vital Speeches of the Day* (July 21, 1983), p. 689.
32. John E. Jacob, "New Realities, New Responsibilities," *Vital Speeches of the Day* (February 1, 1982), p. 255.
33. James D. Williams, ed., *The State of Black America* (Washington, D.C.: National Urban League, Inc., 1986).
34. Jacob, "A Movement That Has Made a Difference," p. 687.
35. Clarence Thomas, "Pluralism Lives: Blacks Don't All Think Alike," *Los Angeles Times* (November 15, 1985), Part II.
36. Fred Barnes, "Farrakhan Frenzy," *The New Republic* (October 21, 1985), p. 14.
37. Linda S. Lichter, "Who Speaks for Black America?" *Public Opinion* (August/September, 1985), p. 42.
38. Id., p. 43.
39. Id., p. 42.
40. Clarence Thomas, "Pluralism Lives," Part II.

6

A New Civil Rights Strategy

In defending their agenda, the revisionists are fond of drawing the analogy of a runner in a race who is shackled to a ball and chain. How can he possibly reach the finish line with such a debilitating handicap?

The revisionists are correct in identifying such an arbitrary, artificial impediment as a civil rights problem. But their proposed solution—to place the handicapped runner at the finish line; or even more regrettably, to cripple the other racers—is utterly incompatible with the basic principles of civil rights. The revisionists overlook the most obvious solution to this problem—to remove the shackles from the disadvantaged runner, and moreover, to dismantle those shackles so as to prevent their use to hinder anyone ever again. This strategy may not necessarily result in the previously burdened runner always winning the race, or even winning his proportionate "share," but will allow him to pursue that objective based solely upon his talent and motivation while retaining self-esteem; and just as importantly, it will forever prevent others from blocking his way.

In crafting a new strategy for the duration of this century and beyond, it is imperative that the first principles of civil rights provide the moral touchstone against which any specific proposal is measured. History makes clear that civil rights have advanced or declined in direct proportion with the nation's commitment to the fundamental principles of individual rights and equality under the law. Indeed, the present crisis that threatens to destroy America's commitment to civil rights is the direct consequence of the movement's abandonment of these principles.

The advocates of civil rights must at the outset bear in mind an important lesson taught by recent history—that the goal of economic progress is important, but it must not displace the principal thrust of the movement, which is to promote individual rights and equal opportunity. The sacrifice of principle to perceived expediency during the last 25 years has made it clear that the quest for material equality as an end in itself is self-defeating and erodes the civil rights consensus. Consequently, while proponents of the traditional civil rights vision may correctly claim that its principles have historically induced greater material equality, the causes and effects should never be confused. Freedom frequently leads to economic progress, but coercion to achieve equality can never lead to freedom.

With this basic understanding, the contemporary civil rights movement can—as its predecessors did—consider the civil rights issues that confront America today, and compose a dynamic, responsive strategy that will eradicate present deprivations and ensure they will not recur.

The issues today are somewhat different than the issues of the past, although they trace their antecedents to the statist ideology that rationalized slavery and Jim Crow. These deprivations take the form of laws and regulations imposed at every level of government that inhibit the right of individuals to conduct their own affairs and control their own destinies. But unlike past violations of civil rights that were explicitly premised on color or ethnic origin, most of the contemporary obstacles are not restricted to any particular race or color. A violation of individual liberty, even if nominally applied to everyone, is nonetheless a violation of civil rights. Not surprisingly, however, these burdens impose their harshest penalties on minorities and the poor, and are no less a matter of civil rights because they are not explicitly premised on race. Indeed, laws neutral on their face may be unequal in effect. As Professor Sowell observes,

> In determining the impact of government on ethnic minorities, it must be recognized that such impact does not depend upon whether government policy is explicitly racial, or even racial in intention, but only on whether its *effects* are different for different ethnic groups.[1]

The two most pervasive and debilitating civil rights deprivations currently facing us are easily apparent—specifically, government policies that severely restrict entrepreneurial and educational opportunities. These barriers affect everyone, but their impact is disproportionately inflicted upon minorities and the poor, creating obstacles in some ways greater than those faced by past generations, since the opportunities that are restricted or precluded are precisely the types of opportunities that facilitated many of the economic gains by blacks and other minorities during the past forty years[2]; hence their further erosion may doom future progress. Accordingly, to the extent the civil rights movement can successfully eradicate the barriers that prevent access to these critical opportunities, minorities and the poor can expect to resuscitate and perhaps accelerate the socioeconomic progress they were making prior to the ascendancy of the revised agenda and the welfare state.

Although entrepreneurial and educational opportunity should occupy the central focus of the contemporary new civil rights strategy, that strategy will be incomplete if it fails to confront the cycle of poverty and dependency that stifles the ability of minorities and the poor to take advantage of such opportunities even where they are already available. Just as the abolitionists destroyed slavery, so must contemporary civil rights pioneers seek to create the conditions within which victims of the vicious cycle can escape its confines and effectively exercise their civil rights on an equal basis with all Americans.

A viable, forward-looking civil rights strategy dedicated to these objectives must begin by redefining the terms of the debate. Presently, the debate is focused not on civil rights, but instead on the redistribution of wealth and on other forms of social engineering. In addition to exposing the true nature of the revised agenda, sincere advocates of civil rights must establish their credibility by aggressively challenging those obstacles that stand in the way of the civil rights vision.

The quest for civil rights in America is at a crucial crossroads, and the direction we choose will determine the prospects for civil rights in America's third century. The time has come for the civil rights movement to pronounce the revised agenda a failure, and to return to the original principles underlying the civil rights vision. The time has come for those who have rightly resisted the revised agenda to recognize that serious civil rights problems exist today, and to pursue a creative, principled, and positive civil rights strategy to surmount these impediments. The time has come for all Americans to realize that civil rights are not simply a matter of concern for one group or another; but that we all share a vested interest in civil rights, an interest that is in grave jeopardy today.

The proposals outlined in the following pages are not intended to exhaust all possible facets of this endeavor, but rather to suggest the parameters for an effective civil rights strategy—they are offered to join the debate, not to settle it; and as a first step in restoring the course of civil rights that was so carefully set more than two centuries ago. America has lost a great deal of ground in the past 25 years; but if the history of the quest for civil rights demonstrates anything at all, it is that a passionate commitment to fundamental principles can overcome nearly any obstacle.

Entrepreneurial Opportunities

Civil rights and economic liberty are intertwined. In a free society, every individual may pursue whatever enterprise he or she wishes, and to succeed or fail according to individual merit, talent, and ambition. Throughout history in the United States and elsewhere, racial tolerance and individual freedom have developed most rapidly in practice and as an ideal in centers of free commerce.³ Conversely, the subjugation of some individuals by others has been most effectively accomplished where the power of the state has been exploited to deny or limit access to such commerce.

Individuals formed societies to safeguard their right to deal with each other on a voluntarily basis. Thus, a society that uses the power of government to restrict voluntary commerce thereby violates the fundamental civil rights of its constituents. Where free trade is completely eliminated, the resulting condition is slavery. In this country, the elimination of slavery was followed by the imposition of a pervasive system of restrictions that limited access to the marketplace on the basis of race and color. Although such express distinctions are now unlawful, the desire by some to limit the access of others to the market has not subsided. The forms of state-enforced coercion utilized to accomplish such ends, however, have become more subtle and sophisticated, yet no less pernicious in motivation or effect. Accordingly, the contemporary civil rights movement must—as did its predecessors—commit itself to eliminating arbitrary economic regulations that deprive individuals of their civil right to pursue enterprises and engage in voluntary commerce. The clear message of history, as Professor Jennifer Roback concluded in her study of market interferences in the Jim Crow era, is that "government, not private individuals, . . . must be restrained in order to allow disfavored minorities to make substantial economic progress."⁴

Economic regulations implicate civil rights in two ways. Where laws arbitrarily restrict an individual's ability to pursue an enterprise, they constitute an infringement of the individual liberty that is the essence of civil rights. And where such laws arbitrarily limit participation in a particular occupation to a certain number or group, they violate the principle of equal opportunity under the law. As Milton Friedman observes, the principles of individual freedom and equal opportunity translate into an economic policy of "free enterprise, competition, laissez-faire. Everyone [is] free to go into any business, follow any occupation, buy any property, subject only to the agreement of the other parties to the transaction."⁵ Such is the economic policy necessary to make civil rights meaningful.

But more than ever before, government at every level has erected barriers to free participation in the marketplace, and a civil rights strategy that ignores such barriers is woefully incomplete. Dr. Walter Williams, an economist whose book, *The State Against Blacks*, provides a comprehensive analysis of these barriers, argues that "those clamoring against quotas assume that the economic game is being played fairly. It is not being played fairly. It is rigged . . . in a way particularly devastating to blacks."⁶ He explains that

> black handicaps resulting from centuries of slavery, followed by years of gross

denials of constitutional rights, have been reinforced by government laws. The government laws that have proven most devastating, for many blacks, are those that govern economic activity. The laws are not discriminatory in the sense that they are aimed specifically at blacks. But they are discriminatory in the sense that they deny full opportunity for the most disadvantaged Americans, among whom blacks are disproportionately represented.[7]

Most interferences with the marketplace are ostensibly benevolent, but their motivations are often arbitrary and their effects debilitating. In his study of the nature and consequence of these policies, Dr. Williams argues that "[w]hat modern Americans have done is resurrect the mercantile system of monopolies and other state privileges that the Founding Fathers sought to escape."[8] This ever-expanding regulatory apparatus threatens to impede, if not destroy, economic opportunity in America; and thus presents an enormous impediment to civil rights. This is particularly true as it concerns blacks, who secured legal assurances of equal opportunity in 1964, but whose victory in that regard will be a pyrrhic one if that opportunity is not extended to the economic realm. Accordingly, the quest for economic opportunity must occupy a central focus in the next generation of the civil rights movement. While the primary benefits of such a strategy will directly accrue to blacks and other minorities, any effort to reduce economic regulation will ultimately benefit all Americans in the form of expanded freedom and opportunity.

Examples of government policies that impede civil rights by arbitrarily limiting economic liberty are numerous. The following are a few of the most burdensome regulations that should be attacked by the contemporary civil rights movement.

Occupational Licensing and Government Monopolies

It took blacks more than two centuries to be granted the same basic rights that most immigrants found immediately upon arrival in America. Yet, even upon attaining equal status under the law, many blacks—and others who are similarly in the early stages of economic development— have discovered government-erected barriers that preclude advancement. Dr. Williams relates that

> there are significant differences in opportunities for upward mobility which blacks face relative to ethnic groups despised and disadvantaged in the past. The major difference is that when other ethnics became urbanized, markets were freer and less regulated. When blacks became urbanized . . . they very often found these avenues of traditional upward mobility closed through various forms of business and occupational regulations.[9]

Occupational licensing laws are an enduring and debilitating relic of the Jim Crow era. Slaves were often well-trained in the crafts and trades, and the white supremacists resorted to licensing laws to prevent them from pursuing such enterprises, thus leaving blacks to work in servile jobs and depriving them of opportunities to escape their caste.[10] In later years, craft unions such as plumbers and electricians advocated licensure laws explicitly to eliminate black competition.[11]

The early civil rights movement viewed licensing with disdain. Between 1892-1907, blacks initiated boycotts against segregated transit in two dozen cities throughout the South.[12] The boycotts persevered because blacks initiated their own transportation companies, thereby introducing competition into the market while providing entrepreneurial opportunities and consumer choice to the black community; but the supremacists countered by charging them with licensing violations.[13] Civil rights advocates understood that entrepreneurial efforts such as their alternative transit companies were precisely what was necessary to gain a toehold in the American economic system, but no legal or political mechanisms existed to help them challenge the restrictions that stymied them. Since the Supreme Court had decided in the *Slaughter-House Cases* that monopoly privileges conferred by government did not constitute a violation of civil rights, white supremacists and others who wanted to maintain their economic positions against black competition repeatedly turned to the coercive apparatus of the state in the form of occupational licensing to restrict opportunities.

In the ensuing years, licensing restrictions have expanded dramatically. Their impact on those outside the economic mainstream is difficult to overstate, for fully ten percent of the labor force today works in licensed occupations.[14] As of 1969, California enjoyed the dubious distinction of regulating occupational entry more pervasively than any other state, requiring licenses for 178 different occupations.[15] In terms of the number of people affected and overall economic impact, state occupational licensing laws constitute a greater regulatory burden than all of the federal economic regulatory programs added together.[16] Yet, despite the fact that such laws preclude access to an enormous segment of the economy the contemporary civil rights establishment, in its disdain for the market, has completely ignored the problem. An alternative civil rights strategy, conversely, must confront arbitrary entreperneurial barriers as a blatant deprivation of individual rights and equal opportunity.

Upon examination, most licensing restrictions are unnecessary in part or in whole, according preferential treatment to those already in the regulated industry while imposing burdens on those seeking entry and on consumers in the form of artificially high prices and reduced competition.

Occupational licensing laws typically result from pressure for state regulations from within the affected industry, ostensibly to protect the public welfare, but in reality to restrict entry into the occupation. John H. Shenefield, an Assistant Attorney General during the Carter administration, explains that while these regulations are nominally enacted "as protection for the public against inferior, fraudulent, or dangerous services and products," this rationale has been applied to extend such restrictions "to occupations that, at the most, only minimally affect public health and safety," such as cosmetologists, auctioneers, taxidermists, and junkyard operators.[17]

As Dr. Williams points out, these laws "discriminate against certain people irrespective of their race," specifically "outsiders, latecomers and [the] resourceless," among whom "because of their history in the U.S., blacks are disproportionately represented."[18] Occupational licensing laws follow a distinct pattern that exacerbates these debilitating effects. First, although the laws are enforced by the coercive power of the state, the regulatory powers are frequently delegated to the affected industries themselves, which of course are self-interested in erecting the most stringent entry barriers possible—barriers that are often quite arbitrary and that have, as former Assistant Attorney General Shenefield charges, "no discernable relationship to public protection."[19] Further, entry restrictions are almost always accompanied by a "grandfather clause,"[20] which allows incumbents to remain in the occupation even if they cannot meet the requirements that exclude newcomers. These clauses expose the true motivation behind such restrictions as self-interest rather than public interest; and where self-interest is promoted through the police power of the state, it constitutes a violation of civil rights.

Like the Jim Crow laws, contemporary licensing requirements are administered in the form of examinations, license fees, and education or apprenticeship requirements. A study by Stuart Dorsey found

> the less educated, blacks, apprentices, and other specific groups are more likely than others to fail written licensing examinations, even though they do not appear to be less able than other workers who are admitted. These results suggest that occupational licensing can restrict the labor market opportunities of groups of workers whose alternatives are already limited.[21]

A case in point is licensing laws for beauticians and cosmetologists in Missouri. As a threshhold requirement for entry into the vocation, the state requires 1,220 hours of formal training or 2,440 hours of apprenticeship under an approved cosmetologist.[22] Thereafter, prospective beauticians and cosmetologists must pass both a practical and a written examination. Although Dorsey's study revealed that in a recent examination blacks passed the *performance* component at the same rate as whites, they accounted for only 3% of those passing the *written* examination, and 21% of those failing it.[23] Thus, as with other licensing requirements, would-be beauticians who are demonstrably competent to serve the public are prevented from doing so because they cannot answer esoteric questions, such as the chemical composition of bones, that appear on typical exam-inations—questions that require not only a mastery of the English lan-guage, but knowledge of anatomy and physics.[24] Dr. Williams concludes that "the written examination acts to exclude applicants, mainly by race, who are just as productive as others evaluated by the practical examina-tion."[25]

Perhaps the most flagrant species of protectionist legislation is taxicab franchising, which prevents thousands of potential entrepreneurs from starting businesses and making a living. Absent regulation, the cost of entry into the taxicab market can be quite low. All that is needed is an automobile, which can usually be easily financed since the car serves as collateral; insurance; a driver's license; and a modicum of skill. In Wash-ington, D.C., the taxicab industry has virtually open entry, with only safety and insurance requirements and a $25 annual fee.[26] Consequently, the industry provides substantial entry-level business opportunities for blacks and immigrants. Approximately 90% of all Washington cabs are owner-operated, 70% are owned by blacks, and 50% are operated as a supplement to other jobs or by students to support educational expenses.[27]

But the essentially laissez-faire status of the taxicab market in Wash-ington, with its beneficial impact on minority opportunities, is the excep-tion to the rule. Such opportunities are prohibited by law in the vast majority of cities, in which the local taxicab industries have successfully utilized the coercive power of government to stifle competition. In New York City, for instance, a "medallion" is necessary to operate a taxicab, and none have been issued since before World War II. As a result, the market value of the transferrable medallions is $100,000 or more, effectively pre-cluding taxicab ownership as a viable entry-level entrepreneurial oppor-tunity.[28] Nonetheless, as many as 15,000 illegal "gypsy" cabs operate in the ghetto areas, which would otherwise be poorly served because of the ar-tificially limited supply of licensed cabs, whose drivers can afford to restrict their activities to the more affluent sections of the city.[29] In Philadelphia, taxicabs are regulated by the Public Utilities Commission, which issues licenses for only $20. But the applicant must demonstrate "public con-venience and necessity," which operates as a virtually insurmountable barrier since existing companies employ lawyers solely for the purpose of contesting applications. Consequently, the actual cost of a transferrable license is $20,000, again artificially restricting entry.[30]

The effect of taxicab licensing in terms of lost opportunities is staggering. The relatively free market taxicab industry in the District of Columbia offers low prices and the highest number of cabs per capita of any major city. Washington has 12 cabs per 1,000 people, while New York has only 2.5 and Philadelphia only .3. Moreover, while nearly two thousand blacks own cabs in Washington, only 14 blacks own cabs in Philadelphia.[31] The taxicab franchise laws that exist in most cities across the country are a microcosm of the adverse effects that licensing restrictions needlessly impose upon the entrepreneurial opportunities of blacks and other minorities. The interests purportedly served by licensing laws can often be achieved by less burdensome mechanisms. Laws against fraud, combined with tort liability, can protect public welfare and safety without the adverse effects of unnecessary and arbitrary market restraints. And licensing laws simply aren't worth the enormous costs, which are borne by many to benefit the few. Consumers, of course, pay higher prices due to artificial restraints on the supply of the regulated goods and services. More significantly, countless private sector employment and entrepreneurial opportunities are lost. These restraints are possible only through the power of the state, invoked by some to diminish the rights and opportunities of others. The civil rights movement should use every means at its disposal to expose the fraudulent justifications underlying many of these laws in an effort to limit their scope—and when they are unrelated to some compelling justification, to eradicate them altogether.

Given the pervasiveness of these economic barriers and the strength of the economic interests behind them, this effort could be long and difficult. Thus, in addition to resisting and repealing such laws in particular instances, civil rights advocates should press for federal and state legislation to protect and promote economic liberty, taking up where earlier civil rights laws left off. Specifically, an Economic Liberty Act would prohibit governmental entities at every level from enacting laws or regulations that impede entry into businesses or vocations, or otherwise frustrate equal entrepreneurial opportunities, absent strong justifications. Such a law would eliminate the most pernicious market barriers that hamper opportunities, particularly for minorities and the poor, thus providing a mighty weapon for the civil rights arsenal. Just as importantly, efforts of this nature would help to restore the civil rights movement's appropriate emphasis on fundamental rights and equal opportunity, the absence of which has allowed governmentally erected economic barriers to proliferate without opposition in recent years to the substantial detriment of individual freedom.

Minimum Wage Laws

A favorite technique of those who have sought to frustrate economic progress of blacks and other minorities has been minimum wage laws, which limit economic opportunity behind a benevolent facade. In reality, minimum wage laws consign many individuals to unemployment and poverty, and thus their costs far outweigh any marginal benefits.

The history of minimum wage requirements is sordid. As University of Massachusetts professor Simon Rottenberg explains, "[l]egal minimum wages are frequently an instrument employed by privileged classes of workers to enforce their privileged positions by preventing other classes of workers from entering their occupations and competing with them."[32] Minimum wages reinforce discriminatory practices that a free market would penalize by imposing higher labor costs on those employers who indulge their irrational predilections. Thus, they have been and remain a favorite tool of white supremacists seeking to destroy opportunities for minorities who offer their labor at competitive rates. For instance, in 1908, the racist Brotherhood of Locomotive Firemen, frustrated in their attempts to prevent the hire of black workers by means of a violent strike, instead successfully negotiated an equal pay requirement. "If this course of action is followed," the union predicted, "the incentive for employing Negroes is . . . removed [and] the strike will not have been in vain."[33] Similarly, white unions in South Africa today support such laws for the same purposes.[34] Wherever minimum wage laws exist, they circumscribe freedom of contract, a critical element of civil rights.

The principal justification for minimum wage laws is the "sweat-shop fallacy"—the notion that but for such laws, the nation's workers would be reduced to the bleak working conditions of the Industrial Age. But this implicitly paternalistic assertion overlooks a crucial point—how "benevolent" is it to substitute a low-paying job with no job at all? Countless immigrants started off in entry-level jobs that enabled them to successfully develop work habits and skills and to save so their children could enjoy a better life. By destroying a critical facet of the freedom of contract, minimum wage laws are rapidly erecting a barrier to market entry and eliminating the ability of minorities and the poor to climb the rungs toward the American Dream. A society founded for the protection of civil rights demands that individuals be allowed to determine whether it is better to work for a low wage than not to work at all—and not to have that decision imposed upon them.

Two principal laws impinge upon the freedom to bargain over wages. The Fair Labor Standards Act, passed in 1938, imposes minimum wages and maximum hours. The Davis-Bacon Act, passed in 1931, requires contractors in federally funded construction projects to pay "prevailing" union wages, thus making it difficult for minority contractors to underbid union competitors. Not surprisingly, these laws were motivated in part by racism. The Davis-Bacon Act was supported by white supremacists such as Rep. Clayton Allgood, who resented the "cheap colored labor . . . that is in competition with white labor throughout the country."[35] The ongoing ramifications of this law are apparent even to many who have little use for the free market. The National League of Cities, for instance, has called for repeal of the Davis-Bacon Act, charging that it "artificially forces pay up" and "adversely affects women and minorities."[36] Similarly, the *New York Times* recently advocated eliminating the minimum wage, arguing it penalizes "young, poor workers, who already face formidable barriers to getting and keeping jobs."[37]

By limiting freedom of contract, minimum wage laws are "perverse in their effects," charges Professor Rottenberg. "On the surface," he explains, "they will appear to many to raise the wages of the working poor. Scratch the surface, and it can be seen that such laws can have opposite consequences."[38] The principal consequence, of course, is unemployment: jobs that simply cannot justify minimum wages, such as ushers in movie theaters or baggers in grocery stores, simply disappear—along with the opportunities for entry into the labor market they once provided. Likewise, such laws encourage mechanization, which also leads to the elimination of marginal jobs. And added to the cost of minimum wages are other governmentally mandated expenses such as unemployment insurance, Social Security, and other taxes; and as these hidden costs of employing people rise, so does unemployment.[39]

Minimum wage laws impose their harshest burdens on young people and minorities who lack competitive job skills; and they destroy entry-level and apprenticeship jobs that build human capital.[40] As economist Llad Phillips observes, "[y]oung blacks have been particularly hard hit," with minimum wages literally "driving them from the work force."[41] The results are devastating—black youth employment, which was at one time *lower* than white youth unemployment, is now two times greater, and three to five times higher than the unemployment rate for the general labor force.[42] The following chart[43] illustrates that increases in the minimum wage have coincided with spiraling youth unemployment, particularly among blacks:

Year	White Youth Unemployment	Black Youth Unemployment
1952	10.9%	8.0%
1956	11.2%	15.7%
1963	17.8%	27.0%
1974	16.2%	39.0%
1980	18.5%	37.7%

Thus, the ultimate consequence of this misguided government benevolence may well be the creation of an entire dispossessed generation that will forever remain outside the American economic system.

The civil rights movement must once again dedicate itself to restoring freedom of contract so that individuals can determine their own destinies. A key part of the solution is to eliminate the minimum wage and other laws that limit the ability of individuals to freely bargain in their self-interest, and to create additional legal bulwarks, such as an Economic Liberty Act, to further protect these rights.

This nation was founded by individuals who believed only they—and not government—were competent to govern their own affairs. If the civil rights movement can successfully help America rediscover this fundamental premise, it can help restore those basic opportunities that were traditionally a hallmark of our economic system, thus moving our nation a bit closer to fulfilling the promise of civil rights.

Enterprise Zones

Another reason for the decline in economic opportunities is that government has taxed and regulated enterprises out of business, and these same burdens frustrate the creation of new enterprises. The individual's right to govern his or her own destiny is meaningful only to the extent to which the market—which is the collective expression of individuals pursuing their values—is free.

A first step in lifting the yoke of government from economic opportunity is to concentrate on those areas most ravaged by government interference, i.e., to unleash the free enterprise system in urban America. This can be accomplished through "enterprise zones," or as Secretary Samuel R. Pierce, Jr. of the Department of Housing and Urban Development calls them, "targets of opportunity—areas that are economically dormant but that can be revitalized if all levels of government reduce regulatory burdens and red tape, [and] lower or eliminate excessive taxes."[44]

Thus far, twenty state governments have established 1,300 enterprise zones, providing new and/or existing businesses with investment and "per-employee" tax credits; exemptions from or reductions of sales, use, and capital gains taxes; and exemptions from building codes and air quality standards. In the sixteen states that have had them for a year or more, enterprise zones have attracted more than $3 billion in capital investment and saved or created more than 80,000 jobs.[45] Secretary Pierce believes that enterprise zones will permit "the free enterprise economy [to] marshal its most important asset, its entrepreneurial spirit, and conquer the twin problems of unemployment and economic distress."[46] More importantly, they will create an environment in which individuals can exercise their liberty to form enterprises, provide jobs, and make money.

The economic blight that afflicts our cities, contrasted with the renaissance that occurs when regulatory burdens are lifted or reduced, demonstrates that interferences with the market invariably deprive minorities and the poor of the basic economic opportunities so vital to freedom. Indeed, most of the problems faced by blacks and poor people today can be traced to government barriers that impede individual rights—particularly freedom of contract—and equal economic opportunity. These should be matters of great concern to a sincere, compassionate civil rights movement. Reducing such barriers as occupational licensing and minimum wage laws while creating enterprise zones and bolstering freedom of contract—as matters of civil rights—are a beginning. The bottom line of all these proposals, of course, is to unleash the free enterprise system and the opportunities it provides. America's doctrinal commitment to a free economy has stood as a beacon of opportunity to oppressed people everywhere. And far from merely "trickling down," the effects of economic liberty have consistently flowed directly to the hardest-working and most enterprising among us, regardless of their socioeconomic starting point.

The time has come for the civil rights movement to focus its energy on guaranteeing economic liberty; to become the "new abolitionists," dedicated to eradicating the arbitrary impediments that separate people from opportunity. For economic freedom is every American's birthright—every American's *civil* right.

Educational Opportunities

The American educational system also implicates both individual rights and equality under the law. Education is not in and of itself a civil right, just as there is no civil right to a job. But the essence of civil rights is that every individual possesses the authority to control his or her own destiny. In modern society, the pursuit of education is critically important in exercising fundamental rights. Thus, any arbitrary interference with the pursuit of education constitutes a deprivation of civil rights. Moreover, as the Supreme Court observed in *Brown v. Board of Education*, the principle of equality under the law requires that education, "where the state has undertaken to provide it, . . . must be available to all on equal terms."[47]

The denial of educational liberty stands as one of the most flagrant and crippling violations of civil rights today. The principal source of this deprivation is the monopoly public school system, which limits opportunities for alternative types of education on the one hand while allocating benefits unequally on the other.

Education is the primary mechanism for upward social mobility for minorities and the poor, a fact that makes educational freedom and equal opportunity all the more important. Historically, the civil rights movement consistently emphasized the importance of education as a prerequisite to the meaningful exercise of individual rights and participation in society. Immigrant groups, most notably Jews, repeatedly managed to circumvent prejudices by securing valuable skills through education.[48] Gunnar Myrdal recognized forty years ago that "[w]hat is needed is an education which makes the Negro child adaptable to and moveable in the American culture at large. . . . And he needs it more than the white child, because life will be more difficult for him."[49]

Although revisionists such as Christopher Jencks have denigrated the importance of education in ameliorating the condition of the underclass,[50] and notwithstanding that the agenda of the contemporary civil rights establishment values proportional representation much more highly than educational freedom or quality, it is more clear today than ever before that educational opportunity is a vital prerequisite for those outside the economic mainstream to have any real hope of progress. A recent study revealed, for instance, that teenagers with low educational achievement are several times more likely to become unwed parents, and are severely disadvantaged in the labor market.[51] On the other hand, Charles Murray found that in 1963-65, individual blacks earned 23% higher wages for each extra year of schooling beyond the average for all blacks.[52] Similarly, Thomas Sowell observes that the incomes of blacks with strong family ties and good education parallel that of similarly situated whites; in fact, for more than a decade, incomes for young college-educated black couples outside the South have *exceeded* incomes for comparable whites.[53] Smith and Welch, in their study of black economic progress during the past forty years, concluded unequivocally that "[t]he safest and surest route to permanent black economic mobility lies in additional education in a good school."[54]

As in other areas, the prevailing orthodoxy of the revised agenda with respect to education is under assault within the black community. In their recent article on the pathology of the black underclass, Jeff Howard and Ray Hammond observed that

> three decades after *Brown v. Board of Education*, there is pervasive evidence of real problems in the intellectual performance of black people. . . . Intellectual underachievement is one of the most pernicious effects of racism, because it limits the people's ability to solve problems over which they are capable of exercising substantial control.[55]

Howard and Hammond's proposed solution is for blacks to place a higher value on intellectual achievement and "assume responsibility for our own performance and development."[56] But such aspirations are often rendered futile by the monopoly public education system, within which many poor and minority children—and their dreams and prospects—are held hostage. As Milton Friedman charges, "[t]he tragedy, and irony, is that a system dedicated to ... giving all children educational opportunity, should in practice exacerbate the stratification of society and provide highly unequal educational opportunity."[57]

From almost any vantage point, the monopoly public school system is a failure. A blue-ribbon presidential commission recently investigated the state of public education and pronounced it abysmal. The commission concluded "the educational foundations of our society are presently being eroded by a rising tide of educational mediocrity that threatens our very future as a Nation and a people,"[58] and grimly predicted that "for the first time in the history of our country, the educational skills of one generation will not surpass, will not equal, will not even approach, those of their parents."[59]

The commission assigned the blame to several deleterious developments in contemporary education. Curricula, for instance, have been "homogenized, diluted, and diffused to the point that they no longer have a central purpose," resulting in a "cafeteria-style curriculum in which the appetizers and desserts can easily be mistaken for the main courses."[60] The typical school provides an average of only four hours of academic instruction per day and requires only one hour of homework per night. Students are increasingly being taught by teachers who ranked in the bottom quarter of their college graduating classes. Discipline problems are often so disruptive that whatever learning environment is possible given other impediments is soon destroyed.

The commission recommended a host of well-meaning reforms, most of them embracing techniques that have been used successfully by private schools for years. But many of the reforms are middle-class solutions whose effects cannot be expected to seep down to those whose schools are more like prisons and houses of ill-repute than institutions of learning. Moreover, some of the reforms, such as substantial pay raises for teachers, in many cases reward mediocrity while inflating costs that are already far too high. Indeed, little apparent correlation exists between spending and educational performance. Alaska and the District of Columbia, for instance, rank first and third in per-pupil expenditures, and have the highest teacher salaries in the nation, but Alaskan students rank only twentieth in educational performance on standardized tests, while District students place fourth from the bottom among jurisdictions using SAT scores. Conversely, New Hampshire ranks twenty-seventh in spending but first in academic performance.[61] Nationally, academic achievement plummeted during the 1970s just as educational expenditures were soaring by 25.2% in inflation-adjusted dollars.[62] Moreover, evidence suggests the much-heralded recent partial rebound in standardized test scores among students nationwide is attributable not to increased expenditures, but in large part to an emphasis on educational basics and to gains by private school students.[63]

The flaws in contemporary American education are thus not a result of too little spending, but are instead symptoms of a deeper malady endemic to the monopoly public school system.[64] This malady can be traced to both the public and monopolistic aspects of the system. The *public* nature of schooling inevitably leads to problems inherent in the public provision of any service. As a matter of course, public education is a political process, which lends itself to special interest pressures. To a large extent, the afflictions of public education—tenure laws, skyrocketing costs, declining standards, incompetent teachers, administrative bloat, inefficiency—are a consequence of the "capture" of public schools by teachers' unions, which utilize their carefully crafted skills to benefit their members through sophisticated manipulations of the political process, at enormous cost to educational quality. In the space of only five years during the 1970s, for instance, the number of students in public schools increased only 1%, but the number of administrators jumped by 44%. No private sector school could afford such bureaucratic surplusage; but as Milton Friedman points out, in the public educational sector, "the producer is in the saddle so the consumer has little to say."[65] This malady is exacerbated by the fact that the public nature of education leaves schools open to third parties to impose their views and values. In this way have public schools been transformed into social laboratories, with schoolchildren as the guinea pigs.

As if these inherent flaws in government provision of education were not enough, their effects are magnified by the quasi-*monopoly* status conferred by the state. The massive burdens of tax financing render it difficult, if not impossible, for most parents to opt out of public education. With both a steady source of funds to which private schools are not privy and a student body held captive by compulsory attendance laws—in essence, artificial supply-and-demand—public schools are subject to virtually no competitive pressure to produce a quality product.

As beween these two critical flaws, the more devastating in terms of educational opportunity is the monopoly privilege enjoyed by public schools. Only in the absence of competition from the private sector can public schools indulge in such luxuries as administrative obesity, inflated salaries, political lobbying, and an often contemptuous attitude toward the concerns of the "owners," the taxpayers. Since none of the current reform proposals address the monopoly issue, they are woefully inadequate in removing the barriers to educational opportunities for those who need them the most.

As with other governmental programs that prevent individuals from controlling their own destinies, the debilitating effects of the public school monopoly are most pronounced among minorities and the poor. The dropout rate for blacks is 30%, in itself cause for grave concern.[66] Recent SAT scores for blacks lagged behind those for whites by more than 100 points in both the verbal and mathematics components.[67] In 1982, only 205 blacks nationwide scored above 700 on the mathematics portion, compared to 3,015 Asian-Americans.[68] That same year, a third of all black sophomores received D's or failing grades in English, and 40% in mathematics—more than twice the percentage for white students.[69] In 1980, the average white young adult read at the tenth grade level, whereas the average black young adult read at only a seventh grade level.[70] Yet, public schools frequently respond not by demanding greater effort but by lowering their standards, reinforcing the stigma of inferiority that has afflicted blacks from slavery through the era of racial preferences. As Professor Loury asks rhetorically, "Is there so little faith in the aptitude of minority ... people that the highest standards should not be held out for them?"[71]

Increasingly, the only prospect many poor and minority children have for a sound education—and hence for inter-generational upward social mobility—is in the private sector; and of course that option is accessible only to a precious few. Attending private schools requires substantial financial sacrifice, and the burden of private school tuition is magnified by the omnipresent obligation to pay taxes for public schools. But more and more parents are making whatever sacrifices are necessary to secure quality education for their children outside the public system. During the past five years, public school enrollment, notwithstanding ever-escalating tax support, has declined by five percent, while enrollment in private schools has increased 7.5%.[72] This movement to private schools is particularly pronounced among minorities and the poor. At least 300 schools operated by and for blacks have been established across the United States.[73] Fully half the students in urban private schools are black, and another third are Hispanic. Moreover, half of urban private school families have incomes of $10,000 or less.[74] The fact that many poor and minority parents commit a substantial portion of their family incomes to send their children to private schools as opposed to "free" public schools underscores how highly they value the educational opportunities the private sector provides.

For those willing and able to make such an investment, the returns are generally most impressive. Unlike public schools, private schools must be extremely productive, competitive, and responsive to parental demands in order to survive. Private schools typically meet this challenge in three principal ways: through greater educational expectations, with an emphasis on basic skills, rigorous academic courses, and more hours of homework;

an orderly learning environment buttressed by stringent disciplinary standards; and operational efficiency, eschewing the bureaucratic malaise that permeates the public sector. The most successful of the public schools also exhibit these characteristics; but in the private sector, they are not optional or experimental, but rather the very keys to survival. These time-proven methods enable private schools, particularly in the inner city, to offer superior educational opportunities at a fraction of the actual cost of public schools.

The impact of private schools on academic success is often substantial, particularly for minority youngsters. Private school students score well above the national average in every academic area. Black private school students in recent SAT tests outscored their public school counterparts by 44 points on the verbal section and 28 points in mathematics.[75] Recent studies found that black students in private schools exhibit far greater discipline and self-esteem and develop higher social and educational aspirations than their public school counterparts. Perhaps most significantly, private schools enhance upward social mobility. As sociologist Andrew Greeley concluded in his study of Catholic schools and minority students, such schools tend to "eliminate . . . the effect of parental social class on academic achievement, a finding as rare in educational research as it is striking."[76] What this means is that private schools can succeed—where mechanisms such as welfare and busing have failed—in providing the tools by which minorities and the poor can escape the shackles of poverty.

This revelation should not be terribly startling, for generations of immigrants and outsiders, including many nineteenth century blacks inspired by Booker T. Washington, successfully pursued education—often in private schools—to lift themselves out of the underclass.[77] Perhaps the most compelling testimony to the opportunities provided by the private educational sector is when public school teachers—certainly among the most "informed consumers"—are 50-100% more likely than their parents to send *their own* children to private schools.[78] Even elected state officials are beginning to buck the National Education Association in recognizing the necessity of educational choice. A recent governors' task force on education concluded, "Schools that compete for students, teachers and dollars will by virtue of their environment make those changes that allow them to succeed. . . . There is nothing more basic to education and its ability to bring our children into the twenty-first century than choice."[79]

These lessons plainly have escaped the contemporary civil rights establishment, however, whose commitment to the failed monopoly public education system is undiminished, and whose reluctance to support efforts to provide impoverished minorities with opportunities to obtain the tools by which they may determine their own destinies is nothing less than shocking. Again, the establishment is out of step with its constituency. Opinion polls show that while a majority of all Americans support increased choice between public and private schools, support is highest among low-income and black parents.[80]

An effective civil rights movement must address itself to those barriers that separate many in our society from educational opportunities. In most cases, the barrier is a financial one; and to the extent the barrier is artificially erected by government, it presents a civil rights issue. The solution is not more money—as earlier discussed, increased funding does not produce better results; and in any event, taxation is never a civil rights "solution" since it requires taking the property of one person to redistribute to another. Rather, the solution, from a civil rights perspective, is to eliminate the government-created monopolistic stronghold of the public educational sector and restore freedom of choice so that individuals can make decisions in their own best interests.

Mechanisms by which to expand educational choice are limited only by the boundaries of creative imagiation, but the two that appear most feasible and meaningful are vouchers and tuition tax credits. Both merit support from advocates of civil rights.

These two methods differ in several respects. Vouchers assume the continued mandatory public financing of education, but would divide that funding into proportionate shares, which would be dispensed for parents to redeem at the public or private school of their choice. Tax credits, conversely, would refund to parents who choose private schools some or all of their tax liability that would otherwise be earmarked for public school support.[81] To benefit those who do not pay sufficient taxes to receive credits, the refund could be extended to non-parent taxpayers, such as relatives or corporations, who could provide scholarships to poor children.[82] Either way, the overall tax burden will be reduced to the extent parents opt out of the public sector, since private schools educate their students at 50-75% of the cost of public schools.

As with any major change in public institutions, increased educational freedom would cause some dislocation (albeit most severely among the ranks of educational bureaucrats and incompetent teachers who would be suddenly unemployed, which accounts for their frenzied opposition to any measure of educational choice). But the most common criticisms levelled against vouchers and tax credits are easily answered.

The most frequent claim is that vouchers and tax credits, as the National Urban League charges, would "undercut public education"[83]—an effective scare tactic because many people passionately, if misguidedly, support the public school monopoly. But this objection reflects confusion over means and ends—public education should be viewed as a *means* to achieve the goal of educational opportunity, not as an end in itself. If a more efficient and effective system can be devised to produce educational opportunity, that should not be a cause for alarm. In any event, however, neither vouchers nor tax credits would likely destroy public schools. Parents who prefer public schools would be free to continue to patronize them. Thus, only those schools that are inefficient and unable to attract students would go out of business, and under such circumstances they deserve to do so; their places will be taken by more responsive private schools. The good public schools, however, have nothing to fear from competition, and even the bad ones will enjoy such competitive advantages as tradition, existing physical plants, and convenient locations. The likely net effect of vouchers and tax credits is that public schools will be forced to shake off generations of acquired lethargy and concentrate once again on the mission of providing education.

A second criticism is that enhanced choice would result in "skimming" the top students from public schools, leaving nothing but a "dumping ground." But as Walter Williams emphasizes, "it's the absence of 'skimming' and . . . effective 'dumping grounds' which is precisely part of the problem,"[84] as public schools over-extend themselves by trying to educate every kind of student. Part of the beauty of the market is that it responds to consumer demand; and an education market free from vice-grip of the public school monopoly can be expected to provide services tailored to every individual need.[85] Moreover, the expectation that serious students would leave others behind if given the option to do so is certainly no argument for holding them hostage in schools that fail to educate them. Educational freedom would make no youngsters worse off, but would provide for the first time a real chance for many to improve their prospects.

Third, opponents of educational freedom contend the primary beneficiaries of vouchers and tax credits would be religiously supported schools, violating the First Amendment's prohibition against establishment of religion. Religious schools presently comprise a major portion of all private schools in large part because their churches subsidize their secular educational programs, thus enabling the schools to partially compensate for their present competitive disadvantage. Once greater competition is possible within the educational marketplace through vouchers or tax credits, secular private schools can be expected to flourish as more parents are able to choose them for their children.

Moreover, the primary effect of efforts to broaden educational choice is not to advance religion, but to expand educational opportunity. The Supreme Court recognized this rather obvious conclusion in the landmark *Mueller v. Allen* decision in 1983, upholding a Minnesota statute providing a modest tax deduction for private or public educational expenses. Writing

for a 5-4 majority, Justice Rehnquist reasoned the First Amendment prohibition "simply [does] not encompass the sort of attenuated financial
benefit, ultimately controlled by the private choices of individual parents,
that ultimately flows to parochial schools."[86] The Court concluded the
deduction "plainly serves [the] purpose of ensuring that the state's citizenry
is well-educated."[87] The *Mueller* decision opens the way for other efforts
designed to promote expanded private sector educational opportunities
through vouchers or tax credits.

Finally, critics charge that private schools promote segregation. In reality, as discussed earlier, private schools, particularly in urban areas, tend to
be more integrated than their public school counterparts, both racially and
socioeconomically. Whereas divisive programs like busing exacerbate such
petty differences as race and economic status, quality education helps
make such differences less noteworthy.

Vouchers and tax credits have not yet been given a full hearing in any
jurisdiction. Minnesota, however, has been the leader in providing educational choice. In addition to its tax deduction program, it has an "early-
exit" law allowing high school students to enroll in classes at public and
private colleges and universities, and Governor Rudy Perpich has proposed
a public sector voucher-type program permitting students to choose from
among any public school in the state.[88] While limited in scope, these measures will promote increased competition, choice, and opportunity—and
hence, civil rights.

Indeed, more important than the improved prospects for socioeconomic
advancement arising from these proposals is the principle of educational
freedom itself. One of the great ironies of our time is that a society that
would rebel at the notion of government telling us which supermarket to
patronize complacently acquiesces when the state instructs us where to
educate our children. The civil rights movement must commit itself to
tenaciously challenging every barrier that impedes educational liberty. The
vested interest in the educational status quo is sizable and growing, but it
leaves out many among those who should be its beneficiaries—the children
themselves. Vouchers and tax credits should form the cornerstone of the
quest to restore to all individuals the civil right to control their own destinies through whatever opportunities are available to them.

The New Slavery

One of the primary objectives of the civil rights movement during the
1960s was integration. But with the frenzied expansion of the welfare state
from the mid-1960s on, overzealous government benevolence created exactly what Franklin Roosevelt and others had warned against—a class of

people separated from mainstream America, with little prospect of ever bridging the ever-widening chasm. The revised agenda transformed the goal of integration into the reality of isolation.

Thus, in addition to the barriers to entrepreneurial and educational opportunities described earlier, many in our society are further shackled by a pervasive, demoralizing cycle of poverty, dependency, and despair. As the failure of the Great Society made clear, no amount of government spending will cure the problem; only those incarcerated within the cycle can fully liberate themselves, and it takes much more time to escape dependency than to succumb to it. To the extent government programs reinforce the vicious cycle, they present issues of civil rights. What is necessary to eradicate this new slavery is nothing less than a second Emancipation Proclamation, directed at abolishing the authoritarian, all-encompassing network of misguided government programs and policies that prevent so many individuals from exercising their rights and enjoying the fruits of a free society.

This does not and cannot mean an immediate end to "safety net" welfare programs. So long as government keeps in place those obstacles to entrepreneurial and educational opportunities that frustrate civil rights and the ability of poor people to improve their condition, it would be disastrous to eliminate programs designed to ameliorate the condition of the victims of those policies. What *is* immediately necessary is a *mea culpa;* an admission that government is not a solution to but a cause of the new slavery, combined with a firm commitment to remove its tentacles from the realm of individual autonomy. Moreover, we should carefully scrutinize all interim welfare programs to ensure that they work as little harm as possible and do not promote dependency at the expense of productive activity. President Reagan recognized the necessity of such a course of action in his "State of the Union" address in January, 1986. The president declared that our task

> is to redefine government's role: not to control, not to command, not to contain us, but to help in times of need; above all, to create a ladder of opportunity to full employment so all Americans can climb toward economic power and justice on their own. . . . [W]e must now escape the spider's web of dependency. . . . I am talking about real and lasting emancipation, because the success of welfare should be judged by how many of its recipients become independent of welfare.[89]

It is, of course, one thing to comprehend the problem, and quite another to take the action necessary to solve it.

The consequences of the new slavery and its roots in government interferences with individual autonomy are now well-chronicled, but nowhere more vividly than in Charles Murray's *Losing Ground.* The thesis of Murray's book is simple—individuals respond to incentives and disincentives; for instance, if government provides an acceptable substitute to work, such as welfare, it will induce many individuals not to work. Proceeding from this thesis, the book explores the disastrous consequences of the misdirected incentives provided by the welfare state.

Murray traces the present predicament to the fundamental policy shift during the early 1960s from an emphasis on opportunity to a quick-fix effort to artificially produce equality in result. The trade-off, as Murray describes it, required abandoning "those methods which have historically proven successful—self-reliance, work skills, education, business experience," in favor of "methods that are more immediate—job quotas, charity, subsidies, preferential treatment," which "tend to undermine self-reliance and pride of achievement in the long-run."[90]

This policy metamorphosis produced disastrous changes in the behavior of those to which it was directed, particularly poor blacks. While many blacks continued to exploit traditional mechanisms to climb the rungs of upward social mobility, and a few—particularly among the most talented and capable—advanced at an accelerated rate via preferential treatment, others were lured into patterns of self-destruction. By 1968, the dependency mentality had firmly taken hold, especially among many young blacks, and welfare dependency, which had been rapidly declining until 1965, began to grow steadily.[91] Murray recounts that "large numbers of young black males stopped engaging in the fundamental process of seeking and holding jobs."[92] The labor force participation rate for young blacks declined alarmingly, and many left the labor market at the early stages of career development—the very time at which skills, work habits, and a work record must be attained—thus virtually forfeiting future prospects for economic independence.[93]

Massive welfare spending also created an entrenched bureaucracy with a vested interest in the expansion of dependency. That bureaucrats are the prime beneficiaries of welfare is illustrated by the fact that although direct payments of $11.4 billion would lift everyone above the poverty level, America spends more than $30 billion annually on welfare, yet five million Americans remain in poverty.[94] As President Reagan charges, "After hundreds of billions of dollars in poverty programs, the plight of the poor grows more painful. But the waste in dollars and cents pales before the most tragic loss—the sinful waste of human spirit and potential."[95] By transforming welfare from a privilege into a "right," government removed the shame associated with welfare and rendered it an acceptable lifestyle, increasing the likelihood that it will be handed down from one generation to the next. A Brookings Institution study found a strong correlation between welfare parents and their children in attitudes toward welfare, the work ethic, aspirations, and levels of confidence.[96] In particular, the study revealed that "welfare mothers are transmitting to their sons a greater tolerance of government support" and "may be hindering their sons' entrance into the work force."[97]

This phenomenon is cause for grave concern that even if barriers to opportunity are eradicated, those locked inside the cycle of poverty will be unable to escape. This worrisome possibility is reflected in the fact that although the economic growth policies of the Reagan administration have produced a large number of new entry-level jobs—many of them paying above minimum wage—a large segment of the unemployed poor is unable or unwilling to fill them.[98] The juxtaposition of a shortage of unskilled labor alongside continuing widespread unemployment among minority youth is one of the cruelest and debilitating ironies of the cycle of poverty. The prospect of a permanent underclass, rendered immune from opportunity, is thus upon us for the first time in history.

Yet another manifestation of the new slavery is the destruction within the black underclass of the family unit, the principal mechanism for support, stability, and the transmission of values. While blacks with strong family ties and educational backgrounds have already attained the same median standard of living as whites,[99] a stable nuclear family unit is increasingly not the norm for many blacks. This breakdown in the family institution can be directly traced to the perverse system of incentives produced by the revised agenda and the welfare state. In 1960, 7.4% of families with children were headed by women without a husband present; today, after two decades of massive government intervention, that figure has increased to 19% overall, and to a debilitating 49% among blacks.[100] Similarly, the illegitimacy rate for blacks is a staggering 56%.[101] This combination is a recipe for perpetual despair, evidenced by the fact that female-headed families account for 56% of those in poverty.[102] Government must immediately and irrevocably eliminate disincentives to family ties.

The disastrous record of the past two decades demonstrates that government programs are ineffective—if not counterproductive—in producing economic equality. What was intended to be a safety net has evolved into an interwoven tapestry that suffocates rather than sustains its dependents. Instead, what government can and should do is to stop trying to ensure economic parity and to instead concern itself with establishing the conditions that will allow individuals to rise to the limits of their own talents and ambition. The task of escaping the underclass is a difficult one, as countless generations have discovered, but there are no shortcuts. On the contrary, the task is now more difficult because poor people today must break out of the habit of dependency before they can even begin climbing the steps of socioeconomic progress—the entry to which is frequently blocked by the governmentally erected barriers described earlier.

These problems require a synthesis of past approaches, combining a frontal assault on the *system* of civil rights deprivations, in the tradition of W.E.B. DuBois and Martin Luther King, with a conscious effort by blacks to escape the pathology of dependency, in the tradition of Booker T. Washington. The first is a civil rights strategy; the second a prerequisite to the enjoyment of those rights, and a matter addressable only by blacks and others subject to the yoke of the new slavery. As Glenn Loury urges, "It is absolutely vital that blacks distinguish between the fault which may be attributed to racism as a cause of the black condition, and the responsibility for relieving that condition."[103] Only within the underclass itself do people have a personal stake in their own advancement, and thus they must take the ultimate responsibility for moving forward. America, however, must give them the opportunity to succeed or fail that is the birthright of every citizen.

In addition to the welfare state, another integral component of the vicious cycle about which government should take action as a matter of civil rights is crime. The primary purpose for which societies are formed is to ensure security for fundamental rights. But our government is failing in this task to such an extent that a fundamental reordering of priorities is necessary. Ironically, those who suffer the greatest diminution of fundamental rights—minorities and the poor—also bear the greatest brunt of government's failures with respect to security. Equally remarkable is the paucity of discussion about crime among the contemporary civil rights establishment, except to bolster demands for yet additional social programs to further expand the cycle of dependency. The crime problem must be confronted directly, for security is a necessary pre-condition to the effective exercise of civil rights.

Statistics are useful in illustrating the magnitude of the crime problem, particularly among minorities and the poor. As Charles Murray reveals, since the genesis of the Great Society, murders have increased by 122%, robberies by 294%, burglaries by 189%, and auto thefts by 128%.[104] In 1982, the probability of being murdered was six times greater for blacks than whites. Blacks account for more than 40% of prison inmates.[105] Moreover, ghetto residents pay 5-20% more for food and other goods, which Whitney Young blames on "exploitation by ghetto merchants,"[106] but which in fact is attributable to dramatically higher security and insurance costs,[107] as well as to diminished competition as many entrepreneurs refuse to do business in neighborhoods that are virtual war zones.

A successful campaign against crime requires both a carrot and a stick. If legal opportunities are artifically diminished, illegal opportunities become more attractive; if the minimum wage prevents someone from earning a loaf of bread, he may feel inclined to steal it. Thus, one side of the crime problem is to remove restraints on honest entrepreneurial activities—if we lift the burdens that frustrate individuals in their ambition to do good, less incentive will exist to do bad. On the other hand, the costs of engaging in crime must be increased. Charles Murray provides the example of Cook County, in which during the 1970s, juvenile criminals were arrested an average of 13.6 times before they were finally committed to reform schools; first-time offenders were at almost no risk of punishment whatsoever.[108] Surely we have our priorities confused when we discourage productive activities but allow criminal activities to go unpunished!

The crime issue is complex, and as earlier noted, it is interrelated with other civil rights issues. But we must re-establish security as the primary responsibility of government, just as President Truman's Committee on Civil Rights did forty years ago.[109] And we must begin by reassessing our entire criminal legal system to ensure it is fully responsive to this overriding priority.

One aspect of the criminal legal system merits special attention because it provides a microcosm of the pernicious effects of misguided government policies: the victimless species of crimes—those crimes that are not wrongful in and of themselves like crimes against people and property, but which instead involve conduct that many people find offensive. Foremost among the victimless crime laws, at least in terms of the number of people affected, are drug laws. Whatever the cost to individuals and society of the underlying conduct, the laws themselves are also enormously costly; and like all attempts to proscribe private, voluntary conduct, they are woefully ineffective, and may in fact do more to encourage than to discourage the proscribed conduct. Drug laws cause drastically higher narcotics prices, which in turn provide an enormous financial incentive to create new addicts, induce ghetto entrepreneurs to whom traditional avenues of economic activity are limited to engage in illegal activities,[110] and compel users to resort to criminal activities to pay the artificially inflated costs.[111] One-quarter of all income derived by inner-city black youth is from crime[112]; and 29% of those arrested for drug offenses are black.[113] Moreover, the American Bar Association has estimated that between one-third and one-half of all street crime is "secondary crime," i.e., crime attributable to addicts seeking to support their habits.[114] As such conservative thinkers as William F. Buckley and Milton Friedman have suggested, we should consider whether the costs of drug laws outweigh the benefits; whether the creation of new criminals and real crimes that are the result of drug prohibition—not to mention the diversion of an enormous proportion of scarce police resources away from crimes against people and property—is warranted. One alternative consistent with civil rights principles is a system in which individuals are free to conduct their own affairs, but are held fully accountable for their actions. This would entail, for instance, eliminating the defense available in some states for those who volitionally impair their mental faculties, e.g., through drugs or alcohol, and thereafter commit crimes or injure people or property.

Time and again, history demonstrates that when government attempts to mold society, problems often become worse rather than better. Only free individuals, acting in pursuit of their own self-interest, can maximize societal well-being. A civil rights strategy consistent with the principle of individual liberty cannot guarantee an end to poverty or despair, but it can—and must—apply itself to eradicating those misguided policies that perpetuate and exacerbate poverty and preclude individuals from controlling their own destinies. That, after all, is what civil rights are all about.

Notes

1. Sowell, *Race and Economics*, p. 179-80 (emphasis in original).
2. Smith and Welch, p. 107.
3. Sowell, *Race and Economics*, p. 207.
4. Roback, p. 1192.
5. Milton and Rose Friedman, p. 133.
6. Walter E. Williams, *The State Against Blacks* (New York: New Press, 1982), p. 123.
7. Id., p. 125.
8. Id.
9. Id., p. xvi.
10. Id., p. 92.
11. Id., p. 91. Similarly, arbitrary licensing requirements such as citizenship were imposed during the 1930s to limit competition by Jewish immigrant artisans. Id., p. 96-97.
12. Meier and Rudwick, p. 90-92.
13. Id., p. 98-99.
14. Stuart Dorsey, "The Occupational Licensing Queue," *Journal of Human Resources*, vol. 15 (Summer 1980), p. 425.
15. Bernard H. Siegan, *Economic Liberties and the Constitution* (Chicago: University of Chicago Press, 1980), p. 200-01.
16. John H. Shenefield, "Regulatory Reform: A Program for the States" (unpublished manuscript presented to the Richmond Bar Association, May 17, 1979), p. 3.
17. Id.
18. Williams, *The State Against Blacks*, p. xvi.
19. Shenefield, p. 3.
20. Dorsey, p. 427.
21. Id., p. 424.
22. Id., p. 428.
23. Williams, *The State Against Blacks*, p. 71-72.

24. Siegan, p. 201.
25. Williams, *The State Against Blacks*, p. 72.
26. Id., p. 81-82.
27. Id., p. 81-84.
28. Id., p. 70.
29. Id., p. 77-78.
30. Id., p. 80.
31. Id., p. 85-86.
32. Rottenberg, p. 5.
33. Walter E. Williams, "Minimum Wage/Maximum Folly and Demagoguery," *The Journal/The Institute for Socioeconomic Studies*, vol. 8 (Winter 1983-84), p. 31-33.
34. Rottenberg, p. 5.
35. Williams, "Minimum Wage," p. 33.
36. "League of Cities Adopts Policy Calling for Repeal of Davis-Bacon," *Daily Labor Report* (Dec. 16, 1985), p. A-3.
37. "The Right Minimum Wage: $0.00," *New York Times* (Jan. 14, 1987), p. A26.
38. Rottenberg, p. 6.
39. Williams, "Minimum Wage," p. 23 n.3.
40. See, e.g., Linda Leighton and Jacob Mincer, "The Effects of Minimum Wages on Human Capital Formation," in Rottenberg, p. 171.
41. Llad Phillips, "Some Aspects of the Social Pathological Behavorial Effects of Unemployment Among Young People," in Rottenberg, p. 188.
42. Williams, *The State Against Blacks*, p. 35.
43. Id., p. 38.
44. Samuel R. Pierce, Jr., "State Enterprise Zones: Targets of Opportunity," *First Reading* (October 1985), p. 7.
45. "Enterprise Zones for All," *Wall Street Journal* (Nov. 7, 1985), p. 30.
46. Pierce, p. 7.
47. *Brown, p. 493.*
48. *Sowell, Race and Economics*, p. 171-72.
49. Myrdal, p. 906 (emphasis deleted).
50. Jencks, p. 255-56.
51. William Raspberry, "The Best Preventive Education," *Washington Post* (September 22, 1986), p. A17.
52. Murray, p. 90.
53. Sowell, *Civil Rights: Rhetoric or Reality?*, p. 80-81.
54. Smith and Welch, p. xxix.
55. Jeff Howard and Ray Hammond, "Rumors of Inferiority," *The New Republic* (Sept. 9, 1985), p. 18.
56. Id., p. 21.
57. Milton and Rose Friedman, p. 158.
58. National Commission on Excellence in Education, A *Nation at Risk* (Washington, D.C.: U.S. Government Printing Office, 1983), p. 5.
59. Id., p. 11.
60. Id., p. 18.
61. Lawrence Feinberg, "Private Schools Push District to SAT Gains, *Washington Post* (Feb. 21, 1986), p. B6; Lawrence Feinberg, "Student Test Scores Hold Steady, Dropout Rate Rises, Bennett Says," *Washington Post* (Feb. 11, 1987), p. A6.

62. Valena White Plisko and Joyce D. Stern, eds., *The Condition of Education* (Washington, D.C.: National Center for Educational Statistics, 1985), p. 40.

63. Feinberg articles (note 61). Separate data for public and private school scores are available only in the District of Columbia. Id. While scores by private school students in the District increased by 40 points between 1982-85, scores for public school students declined by three points. Id., p. Bl.

64. For a further consideration of these issues, from which this discussion is partially adapted, see Clint Bolick, "Solving the Education Crisis: Market Alternatives and Parental Choice," in David Boaz and Edward H. Crane, eds., *Beyond the Status Quo: Policy Proposals for America* (Washington, D.C.: Cato Institute, 1985), p. 207-21.

65. Milton and Rose Friedman, p. 156.

66. Howard and Hammond, p. 17.

67. Murray, p. 106.

68. Loury, *Beyond Civil Rights*, p. 7.

69. Plisko and Stern, p. 52.

70. Murray, p. 105.

71. Loury, *Beyond Civil Rights*, p. 12.

72. Lynn Asinof, "Business Bulletin," *Wall Street Journal* (Nov. 21, 1985), p. 1.

73. Joan Davis Ratteray, "One System Is Not Enough: A Free Market Alternative for the Education of Minorities," *Lincoln Review* (Spring 1984), p. 27. See also, Lucy Keyser, "Push for excellence stirs surge of black private schools," *Washington Times* (Jan. 13, 1986), p. 8A.

74. For documentation of statistics on public vs. private schools throughout this section, see James Coleman, Thomas Hoffer, and Sally Kilgore, *High School Achievement* (New York: Basic Books, Inc., 1982); James Cibulka, Timothy O'Brien, and Donald Zewe, *Inner-City Private Elementary Schools: A Study* (Milwaukee: Marquette University Press, 1982); and Andrew Greeley, *Catholic High Schools and Minority Students* (New Brunswick, N.J.: Transaction, Inc., 1982).

75. Murray, p. 255.

76. Greeley, p. 88.

77. For a particularly striking modern-day example, see Marva Collins and Civia Tamarkin, *Marva Collins' Way* (Los Angeles: J.P. Tarcher, 1982).

78. "Governors Opt for Choice of Schools," *Wall Street Journal* (August 28, 1986), p. 14.

79. Id.

80. Id.

81. For a superb debate on the respective merits of vouchers and tax credits, see John E. Coons, "The Voucher Alternative," *Journal of Social, Political and Economic Studies* (Spring 1984), p. 94, and Manny Klausner, "Tuition Tax Credits and the Case Against Government Schools," *Journal of Social, Political and Economic Studies* (Spring 1984). , p. 84.

82. A comprehensive tax credit system is outlined in Bolick, "Solving the Education Crisis," p. 215-17.

83. James Williams, p. 178.

84. Walter Williams, "Inner City Parents and Freedom of Choice," in *Black Education and the Inner City* (Washington, D.C.: Lincoln Institute for Research and Education, 1981), p. 13.

85. See, e.g., "More Pols, Parents Choose Educational Choice," *Reason* (April 1986), p. 21.

86. *Mueller v. Allen*, 463 U.S. 388, 400 (1983).

87. Id., p. 395. For further examination of the significance of the *Mueller* decision, see Clint Bolick, "Private Sector Educational Alternatives and the *Mueller* Decision," *Journal of Social, Political and Economic Studies* (Spring 1984), p. 79.

88. Robert W. Poole, Jr., Lucy Braun, Bill Kauffman, and Eric Marti, "More Pols, Parents Choose Educational Choice," *Reason* (April 1986), p. 20-21.

89. "Text of President's Address to Congress on State of the Union," *Washington Post* (Feb. 5, 1986), p. A20.

90. Murray, p. 238.

91. Id., p. 64-65.

92. Id., p. 78.

93. Id., p. 76, 82.

94. Id., p. 195.

95. President's Address, p. A20.

96. Leonard Goodwin, *Do the Poor Want to Work?* (Washington, D.C.: The Brookings Institution, 1972), p. 65.

97. Id., p. 67.

98. Martha Brannigan, "A Shortage of Youths Brings Wide Changes to the Labor Market, *Wall Street Journal* (September 2, 1986), p. 1.

99. Sowell, *Civil Rights: Rhetoric or Reality?*, p. 80-81.

100. Spencer Rich, "Behind Reagan's Welfare Study," *Washington Post* (Apr. 5, 1986), p. A7.

101. Karl Zinmeister, "The Poverty Problem of the Eighties," *Public Opinion* (June/July 1985), p. 8.

102. Id., p. 9.

103. Glenn C. Loury, "The Moral Quandary of the Black Community," *The Public Interest* (Spring 1985), p. 11.

104. Murray, p. 115.

105. Howard and Hammond, p. 17.

106. Young, p. 40.

107. Murray, p. 176.

108. Id., p. 170.

109. Leon Friedman, p. 3-4.

110. Farley, p. 53.

111. Randy E. Barnett, "Curing the Drug Law Addiction," in Ronald Hamowy, ed., *Dealing With Drugs: The Consequences of Government Control* (Lexington, Ma.; Lexington Books, 1987), p. 73-102. The author expresses his appreciation to the Pacific Research Institute for providing advance review of chapters of this book for use in this discussion.

112. Allan C. Brownfeld, "The Work Ethic and Welfare," *Washington Times* (August 14, 1986), p. 3D.

113. *Uniform Crime Reports for the U.S.* (Washington, D.C.: Federal Bureau of Investigation, 1984), p. 180.

114. Milton Friedman, *There's No Such Thing as a Free Lunch*, p. 228.

7

The Necessity of Judicial Action

The civil rights strategy set out thus far, like its historical antecedents, is quite ambitious, and political action alone is insufficient to implement it. A civil rights movement must proceed simultaneously on every possible front.

Unlike earlier movements, the principles upon which we rely are now firmly established in law. But constitutional and statutory guarantees of civil rights are meaningful only to the extent that a mechanism exists to enforce them. In the American system of government, that vital role is entrusted to the courts.

American history repeatedly illustrates the difficulty in securing civil rights to the extent the judiciary abdicates this role. The abolitionists learned this lesson through the *Dred Scott* decision, just as the post–Civil War civil rights movement learned it through such decisions as the *Slaughter-House Cases* and *Plessy v. Ferguson,* and just as we are learning it yet again through modern-day departures from the principle of equality under the law. Conversely, the great triumphs of the 1950s and 1960s were in large part due to judicial action, which in turn laid the groundwork for further political reform in support of civil rights.

As a practical matter, any effective civil rights strategy must include a focused, aggressive legal agenda.[1] Judicial action lends itself to such a strategy in three important ways. First, judicial action can provide results far more quickly than political action, which usually requires the development of consensus. Principled judicial action, such as in *Brown v. Board of Education,* can precede and in turn inspire such political consensus. Second, legal action can be much "purer" than political action, since court decisions often turn on fundamental principles while politics usually requires compromise. Third, since civil rights are individual rights asserted against the state, the judiciary is the only forum capable of unabashedly safeguarding those rights, for it does not require majoritarian support for its actions. Thus, courts are necessarily the first line of defense for civil rights.

A great deal has already been accomplished in the judicial arena through such decisions as *Brown*, which reversed the infamous "separate but equal" doctrine of *Plessy v. Ferguson*; and in *Bakke* and *Wygant*, which established heightened judicial scrutiny for contemporary forms of state-imposed racial discrimination. But a great deal more remains to be accomplished. The civil rights movement should adopt three primary objectives for its legal program. First, it should seek to establish once and for all the proposition that the Constitution is color-blind, a proposition which despite the efforts of the civil rights movement from the Civil War until *Brown* has never successfully been established as a fundamental maxim of American jurisprudence. Although the "separate but equal" doctrine was reversed by *Brown*, Justice Harlan's dissent in *Plessy* has never been fully adopted by the courts; and until the principle that government may never draw distinctions based upon race and color is firmly established, civil rights will always remain vulnerable to compromise. Second, the civil rights movement should seek to reverse the *Slaughter-House Cases*, which upheld the power of government to create monopolies and impede entrepreneurial opportunities. Until economic liberty is protected, opportunity will remain unequal, with the devastating effects discussed earlier. Finally, the movement should complete another task left unfinished since *Brown*—the eradication of state-imposed impediments to precious educational opportunities.

A movement sincerely devoted to civil rights should be capable of taking effective judicial action once it resolves to do so.* Certainly, the revisionists have successfully used the courts despite their blatantly special-interest objectives and the necessity of distorting the Constitution and statutory law to accomplish them. Though it will take creativity and determination to wrest the judicial forum from the revisionists, the task is not so hopeless as to justify outright capitulation. Indeed, judicial action may provide the surest and swiftest route to the renaissance of the civil rights movement in America.

A Rationale for Judicial Action

The first and perhaps greatest obstacle to crafting a creative and effective civil rights strategy in the courts is the notion, popular among many who

---

*A handful of "public interest" law firms espousing individual rights have been formed in the past decade, but their success to date has been limited by insufficient funding as well as, to varying degrees, inadequate leadership, risk avoidance, co-optation by special interests, and the lack of a principled, coherent long-range vision. Arrayed against those groups are at least 185 "civil rights" advocacy organizations coalesced within the Leadership Conference for Civil Rights and boasting a much more successful track record.

sincerely support the principles of civil rights, that judicial action toward this end is somehow contrary to our system of government. This view is largely a reaction to decades of unfettered judicial abuses, which have given rise to an understandable impulse to retrench rather than to counterattack. But by disavowing vigorous judicial action to vindicate fundamental individual rights, these advocates would deprive the quest for civil rights of a primary and wholly legitimate mechanism for progress, while locking into place an extremely unsatisfactory status quo. Instead, the civil rights movement should proceed simultaneously on two fronts: challenging the revised agenda and the availability of courts to invade, rather than preserve, individual rights; and establishing judicial protection for civil rights against invasions by the state.

Before embarking upon such a course of action, it is necessary to confront two inter-related intellectual bogeymen. The first is that the judiciary must always defer to the popular will, and the second is that it must be guided solely by what is perceived as "original intent." Indeed, the unfettered application of these two notions would emasculate the central role the framers assigned to the judiciary in protecting civil rights. The existence of these bogeymen is a case of disingenuously invoking the framers so as to frustrate their own grand design.

The debate over the proper role of the courts is illustrated by a recent debate between Justice (then Judge) Antonin Scalia and University of Chicago law professor Richard Epstein, who generally agree upon the desired "ends" but not upon the means to accomplish them. Justice Scalia, defending "judicial restraint," concedes the importance of protecting economic liberty, observing that "the difference between economic freedoms and what are generally called civil rights turns out to be a difference of degree rather than kind," and recognizing that "in modern times the demise of economic freedom has been the grave of political freedom as well."[2] Nonetheless, Justice Scalia seems willing to sacrifice judicial protection for economic liberties in order to squelch judicial adventurism, arguing that "the reinforcement of mistaken and unconstitutional perceptions of the role of courts in our system far outweighs whatever evils may have accrued from undue abstention in the economic field."[3] Moreover, he believes it unlikely that judicial adventurism can be curbed "at the same time we are charging forward on an entirely new front."[4] Scalia would thus accord greater deference to the legislative branch.

Professor Epstein counters that Scalia's approach would remove a vital check against legislative abuses. "Our constitution reflects a general distrust toward the political process of government," Epstein argues. By "focusing exclusively on the defects . . . in the judicial part of the process," he warns, Scalia "tends to ignore the powerful defects that pervade the legislative part of the process."[5]

Epstein's view is echoed by University of San Diego law professor Bernard Siegan, whose book, *Economic Liberties and the Constitution*, persuasively demonstrates the necessity of judicial protection for individual rights. Siegan concludes that "[a] judicial system more concerned to protect the power of government than the freedom of individuals has lost its mission under the Constitution."[6] But others fear that aggressive judicial action in defense of individual rights would tacitly sanction the abuses of judicial power that have become commonplace in recent years. Terry Eastland, for instance, argues that "[a]ctivism, once endorsed, can lead in any direction, and there is nothing in an activist philosophy that can prevent the judicial imposition of personal or class-bound sympathies as the law of the land."[7]

This view is seriously mistaken. A principled approach that defines the appropriate line of demarcation between legitimate and illegitimate judicial action can—and must—be articulated. What the advocates of judicial abstinence overlook is the crucial role assigned by the Constitution to the judiciary in the protection of civil rights, without which the state will be free—as in the Jim Crow era—to subvert civil rights virtually unchecked.

Judicial action in defense of civil rights is not a frolic inconsistent with "original intent," but, as Professor Epstein argues, is actually a "necessary implication derived from the constitutional text and the underlying theory of the state that it embodies."[8] The real debate between those who advocate principled judicial action and those who counsel restraint is not whether the Constitution governs the proper role of the judiciary, but rather whether the Constitution primarily protects individual rights or the power of the majority. Thus, most of the advocates of judicial restraint are selective in their interpretation of "original intent," focusing upon the Constitution's majoritarian elements rather than upon limiting principles such as the Ninth and Tenth Amendments, or upon the underlying natural rights principles. As Harvard government professor Stephen Macedo explains, when such proponents of restraint

> treat rights as islands surrounded by a sea of government powers, they precisely reverse the view of the Founders as enshrined in the Constitution, wherein government powers are limited and specified and rendered as islands surrounded by a sea of individual rights.[9]

This view is confirmed by the framers themselves. Madison, in proposing a bill of rights, envisioned that the "individual tribunals of justice" would serve as "the guardians of those rights," providing an "impenetrable barrier against every assumption of power in the legislative or executive" branches inconsistent with those rights.[10] But the keenest insight was provided by Alexander Hamilton, who viewed the Constitution in its entirety and "to every useful purpose" as "A BILL OF RIGHTS."[11] In *The Federalist No. 78*, Hamilton comprehensively defined the constitutional role of the judiciary as precisely the opposite of what it is today—active in defense of individual rights, but deferential to the will of the majority as expressed through the legislature where fundamental rights are not implicated. Hamilton understood that the natural inclination of individuals in power is to expand that power. But while the legislative and executive branches broaden their power at the expense of individual rights, the power of the judiciary is only negative, and can be maximized only by *restraining* the power of the other two branches, i.e., by invalidating legislative or executive actions that exceed constitutional parameters. Thus was the ingenious and delicate constitutional balance of powers devised to safeguard individual rights.

Defined in this manner, Hamilton explained that "the courts of justice are to be considered as the bulwarks of a limited Constitution against legislative encroachments,"[12] and were "designed to be an intermediate body between the people and the legislature, in order . . . to keep the latter within the limits assigned to their authority."[13] Like Paine, Hamilton appreciated the necessity of protecting individual rights against majoritarian passions, and he viewed the judiciary as the guardian of those rights against "dangerous innovations in the government, and serious oppressions of the minor party in the community."[14] All citizens would have a stake in an independent judiciary, Hamilton insisted, since "no man can be sure that he may not be to-morrow the victim of a spirit of injustice, by which he may be a gainer to day."[15] For these reasons, the judiciary was the best possible mechanism to safeguard the rights retained by the people in the constitutional government. As Hamilton observed, "[i]n a monarchy it is an excellent barrier to the despotism of the prince; in a republic it is a no less excellent barrier to the encroachments and concessions of the representative body."[16]

The device by which the judiciary would carry out this responsibility was to strike down government action whenever inconsistent with the Constitution. Hamilton explained the Constitution authorizes and obliges the courts "to declare all acts contrary to the manifest tenor of the Constitution void. Without this, all the reservations of particular rights or privileges would amount to nothing."[17] He elaborated,

> No legislative act . . . contrary to the Constitution, can be valid. To deny this, would be to affirm, that the deputy is greater than his principal; that the servant is above his master; that the representatives of the people are superior to the people themselves; than men acting by virtue of powers, may do not only what their powers do not authorize, but what they forbid. . . . Nor does this conclusion by any means suppose a superiority of the judicial to the

legislative authority. It only supposes that the power of the people is superior to both; and that where the will of the legislature, declared in its statutes, stands in opposition to the will of the people, declared in the Constitution, the judges ought to be governed by the latter rather than the former . . . [i.e.,] by the fundamental laws, rather than by those which are not fundamental.[18]

Hamilton's view was shared by Chief Justice John Marshall, who established in *Marbury v. Madison* the central role of the Supreme Court as the principal defender of rights against governmental abuses in the constitutional system of checks and balances. Marshall declared that the "very essence of civil liberty certainly consists in the right of every individual to claim the protection of the laws, whenever he receives an injury. One of the first duties of government is to afford that protection."[19] Accordingly, he concluded that "an act of the legislature, repugnant to the Constitution, is void."[20] Since the *Marbury* decision in 1803, the quest for civil rights has been most potent when it has successfully invoked the judicial power in the manner intended by the framers—to protect individual rights against government.

Certainly, unfettered and unprincipled judicial power could impede rather than advance civil rights, as illustrated by much of the jurisprudence during the past two decades. Hamilton recognized that despite the critical role of the judiciary in defending fundamental rights, dangers of abuse clearly existed. Although "liberty can have nothing to fear from the judiciary alone," he declared, "it would have everything to fear from its union with either of the other two departments."[21] Hamilton's warning describes the predicament that exists in the courts today—the judiciary has largely abandoned its central role in preserving fundamental rights, while taking unto inself legislative powers to rearrange and redefine those rights. Thus, a principal priority of the civil rights movement in the coming years must be to curb the abuse of judicial power while at the same time restoring the judiciary to its assigned role as the principal mechanism by which to vindicate civil rights. And, as Hamilton's treatise demonstrates, the rationale by which to accomplish this task can be found in the Constitution itself.

Restoring Economic Liberty

As discussed in the preceding chapter, one of the most glaring obstacles to civil rights in America today is the pervasive regulation of economic opportunities by government. These regulations frustrate—and in some cases prohibit outright—opportunities to participate and advance in the American economic system, even insofar as the ability to earn a basic living. Such restrictions are unequal in intent and effect, blatantly benefitting some while burdening those who need such opportunities the most. A frontal assault against arbitrary governmental barriers to economic opportunities must occupy a primary thrust of the civil rights movement in the coming decades, and judicial action can provide a potent weapon.

That judicial action can be particularly well-suited to removing governmental barriers to economic opportunities is underscored by a line of Supreme Court precedents spanning several decades from the 1890s until the New Deal. During this era, the Supreme Court provided significant protection for economic liberty against arbitrary government actions, relying on the plain language of the Fourteenth Amendment, particularly its prohibition against state action that deprives individuals of liberty or property without due process of law.

This philosophy was forcefully set forth by the four dissenters in the *Slaughter-House Cases* in 1872, who protested that the state-imposed slaughterhouse monopoly was invalid under the Fourteenth Amendment as a matter of civil rights. As Justice Field proclaimed, "That amendment was intended to give practical effect to the declaration of 1776 of inalienable rights, rights which are the gift of the Creator, which the law does not confer, but only recognizes."[22] By upholding the state monopoly, Field argued, "the right of free labor, one of the most sacred and imprescriptable rights of man, is violated."[23] Likewise, Justice Bradley protested that "the individual citizen, as a necessity, must be left free to adopt such calling, profession, or trade as may seem to him most conducive. . . . Without this right he cannot be a freeman."[24]

It took until the following decade for the dissenters to prevail, but when they did it signalled the start of a golden era for economic freedom. The vital connection between civil rights and economic liberty was highlighted in *Yick Wo v. Hopkins*, one of the early decisions of this period. The case involved a San Francisco ordinance requiring approval by the Board of Supervisors to operate a laundry and mandating that all laundries be constructed of brick or stone. The ordinance was clearly aimed at Chinese entrepreneurs, whose laundries were predominantly housed in wooden structures. Under the ordinance, 150 Chinese were arrested for violations and 200 were denied permission to operate, despite the fact that many had been in business for twenty years or more and all had obtained certificates of safety under the prior standards. The Court invalidated the ordinance, characterizing it as "a naked and arbitrary power"[25] that rendered laundry operators "tenants at will, under the supervisors, of their means of living."[26] Although the law was "fair on its face and impartial in appearance," it was "administered by public authority with an evil eye and an unequal hand," thus violating the principle of equal protection of the laws.[27] The Court reaffirmed its commitment to the traditional civil rights vision in a profound proclamation of the nexus between economic liberty and individual freedom:

> [I]n our system, while sovereign powers are delegated to the agencies of government, sovereignty itself remains with the people, by whom and for whom all government exists and acts. . . . [T]he very idea that one may be compelled to hold his life, or the means of living, or any material right essential to the enjoyment of life, at the mere will of another, seems to be intolerable in any country where freedom prevails, as being the essence of slavery itself.[28]

The highest expression of these principles—as well as a foreshadowing of their demise—came in *Lochner v. New York* in 1905. By a 5-4 majority, the Court struck down a New York statute setting maximum hours for bakery workers. Justice Peckham declared that whether the law "is or is not repugnant to the Constitution . . . must be determined from [its] natural effect . . . when put into operation, and not from [its] proclaimed purpose."[29] He reasoned "[t]he employee may desire to earn the extra money which would arise from his working for more than the prescribed time, but this statute forbids the employer from permitting the employee to earn it"; and since the "right to purchase or sell labor is part of the liberty" protected by the Fourteenth Amendment, the statute was plainly unconstitutional.[30] Noting that adequate health and safety standards already existed to protect bakery workers,[31] Justice Peckham assailed the paternalism implicit in the statute:

> There is no contention that bakers as a class are not equal in intelligence and capacity to men in other trades or manual occupations, or that they are not able to assert their rights and care for themselves without the protecting arm of the state, interfering with their independence of judgment and action. They are in no sense wards of the state.[32]

Thus did the majority in *Lochner* proclaim the right of the individual to determine his or her own destiny—the essence of civil rights.

But the dissent by Justice Holmes [33] provided the reactionary rationale for judicial abdication in the area of economic liberty that would finally prevail several decades later and that dominates conventional jurisprudential wisdom even today. Holmes charged that "[t]his case is decided upon an economic theory which a large part of this country does not entertain," namely, the "shibboleth" of "[t]he liberty of the citizen to do as he likes so long as he does not interfere with the liberty of others to do the same."[34] On the contrary, Holmes contended, "a constitution is not intended to embody a particular economic theory."[35] Instead, Holmes preferred a "reasonableness" standard,[36] under which almost any invasion of economic liberty—even if it is "injudicious" or "tyrannical"[37]—would be sanctioned.

The ramifications of Holmes' dissent were disastrous. Solicitor General Charles Fried perceptively observes that "Holmes' argument summarizes the source of our modern intellectual difficulties when it contends that the Constitution was not intended to embody a particular economic theory." That "may be true of other constitutions," Fried explains, "but it's not true of ours, which was organized upon very explicit principles of political theory."[38]

The Supreme Court continued to protect economic liberty until the New Deal, during which the Roosevelt appointees ultimately tipped the balance in favor of providing *carte blanche* authority to governmental entities to control economic activities and stifle entrepreneurial opportunities. By 1955, the metamorphosis was complete. In *Williamson v. Lee Optical*, the Court sustained a statute prohibiting opticians from duplicating old or broken eyeglass lenses and from fitting old lenses into new frames without a prescription from a licensed physician. Justice Douglas, writing for the Court, failed to comprehend the connection between civil rights and economic liberty. Even though the "law may exact a needless, wasteful requirement," Douglas ruled, "it is for the legislature, not the courts, to balance the advantages and disadvantages of the new requirement."[39] Douglas pronounced the death knell of one of the proudest chapters of American jurisprudence, declaring "[t]he day is gone when this Court uses the . . . Fourteenth Amendment to strike down state laws . . . because they may be unwise, improvident, or out of harmony with a particular school of thought."[40] Unfortunately, the "school of thought" so casually dismissed by the Court is the very natural rights philosophy upon which the Constitution—as well as the American civil rights vision—is based.

A more recent case illustrates how utterly the Court has abandoned economic liberty, and how dire are the consequences flowing from its abdication. In the 1976 case of *City of New Orleans v. Dukes*, the Court was presented with a classic, arbitrary licensing restriction that erected a barrier to the quintessential entry-level entrepreneurial enterprise—hot dog pushcarts. The plaintiff, Dukes, had operated her pushcart in the French Quarter for several years until a New Orleans ordinance was passed to prohibit such food sales, thus depriving Dukes of her livelihood. But, as most licensing statutes do, the ordinance provided a "grandfather clause" for long-term operators, of which there were only two. The court of appeals struck the ordinance under the Fourteenth Amendment as totally arbitrary and irrational, but the Supreme Court sustained the law, declaring that under the Amendment, "this Court consistently defers to legislative determinations as to the desirability of particular statutory discriminations."[41] At least insofar as the Fourteenth Amendment was concerned, the Court made it clear the state was free to destroy economic freedom with impunity.

Today, no member of the Supreme Court appears willing to revive the *Lochner* doctrine. In fact, many conservatives condemn any such effort. They argue that during the *Lochner* era, the judiciary improperly substituted its will for that of the legislature. But the crucial point they miss is that the Court did so only when the legislature impermissibly substituted *its* will for the fundamental rights of individuals. Any conservative should agree with the proposition, stated by Justice Sutherland in 1932, that "in our constitutional system, . . . there are certain essentials of liberty with which the state may not dispense."[42] If this is true—if our Constitution is not a blanket grant of power to government, but a limitation of its powers, as the framers understood it—then the judiciary must play a central role in safeguarding the precious fundamental liberties we call "civil rights."

We have lost a great deal of ground since *Lochner*, and a creative and principled litigation strategy to restore judicial protection for economic liberty is critically important. But unfortunately, it is simply not presently feasible to premise such a strategy upon an explicit revival of *Lochner*, given the disdain with which that doctrine is viewed by most jurists, both liberal and conservative. Instead, the civil rights movement must rely upon mainstream litigation vehicles while consistently emphasizing the vital nexus between civil rights and economic liberty.

Some evidence exists that the judiciary may be sympathetic to a modified *Lochner* approach. While some commentators believe that substantive rights have been read out of the Fourteenth Amendment altogether, the Supreme Court has recently suggested there are some limits to the deference it is willing to accord to state regulations. Specifically, for the first time since *Lochner*, the Court is looking behind regulations to determine whether they are actually "rational" or "reasonable," rather than simply presuming their validity.[43] Accordingly, the civil rights movement should aggressively challenge barriers to entry and equal participation in the marketplace as violations of equal protection under the Fourteenth Amendment, in tandem with 42 U.S.C. § 1983, which provides a right to sue state or local governments for deprivations of rights "under color of state law."[44]

To the extent such obstacles create disproportionate burdens upon minorities, it may be possible to invoke "strict scrutiny," which typically results in invalidation of the state action. This possibility is limited by the Supreme Court's admonition that constitutional attacks against state action under the Fourteenth Amendment requires proof of intent to discriminate on the basis of race, which is often difficult or impossible to prove.[45]

Nonetheless, many contemporary economic restraints, such as licensing laws, trace their roots to blatantly racist antecedents in the Jim Crow era. At the heart of every barrier to entry lurks an intent to exclude *someone*—itself a violation of the principle of equal protection of the laws—and in many cases that inherently evil motive may be sufficiently tinged with racism to invoke heightened judicial scrutiny.

Apart from the Fourteenth Amendment, the most fruitful mechanism by which to challenge economic barriers today appears to be Title VII of the Civil Rights Act of 1964, which mandates equal opportunity in employment. State and local governments are included within the scope of the law. Under the "adverse impact" construct, it is unnecessary to prove discriminatory intent in order to demonstrate a violation under the act.

Adverse impact has been a favorite device of the revisionists, who have used it to invalidate non-discriminatory private employment practices on the basis of disproportionate effects. To this extent, it is inconsistent with the purposes of the act, which was designed to eradicate actual discrimination against individuals. But where government—which is required by the Fourteenth Amendment to provide equal opportunities—acts to limit employment opportunities, the effect of the policy is relevant in discerning the "intent" of the legislative body in enacting it.

A recent case, *United States v. Town of Cicero*, illustrates this approach. The town required that applicants for fire or police department positions must have lived in the town for three years, or for one year for all other positions. The town was virtually all white, with the consequence that Cicero had never hired a black employee. Concluding that "the ordinances are a barrier to black employment,"[46] Judge Richard Posner of the Seventh Circuit Court of Appeals declared it "the strongest case for violation of Title VII on a 'disparate impact' theory that I have seen."[47] It is to the removal of arbitrary barriers to opportunity that Title VII can be most effectively directed.

Most governmental interferences with economic liberty, however, arise not from the state's status as an *employer*, but as a *regulator* of economic opportunities. Through franchising, licensing, and other forms of economic regulation—and by empowering quasi-governmental entities, often comprised of members of the affected industries, to exercise such powers—government at every level arbitrarily restricts opportunity, most often to the detriment of poor and minority individuals. While Title VII is primarily concerned with discrimination claims arising from a direct employment relationship, some courts have extended its requirements to third parties who control access to the job market. For instance, one court held that Title VII applies to racing commissions, which through their power to issue licenses "have control over the ability of a driver-trainer to race, i.e., earn a living."[48] Moreover, 707(a) extends the act's coverage to "any person or group of persons . . . engaged in a pattern or practice of resistance to the full enjoyment of any of the rights secured by this title." The definition of "person" in Title VII clearly extends to governmental officials and licensing agencies. Although this strategy has not yet been actively pursued in litigation, it offers some prospect for challenging state-sanctioned impediments to economic liberty, including occupational licensing and other types of barriers and regulations. Even under the most stringent Title VII scrutiny, the governmental entity or licensing board would be free to defend its practices by demonstrating their "necessity." But such a standard would surely imperil the most pernicious, self-serving deprivations of economic liberty and afford some measure of opportunity to those who need it the most.

Another potential strategy to secure economic liberty is to turn antitrust laws against governmentally created barriers and restraints.[49] Whatever their perverse effects, the antitrust laws, if properly construed and applied, can provide strong protection for economic liberty. As Justice Thurgood Marshall declared,

> Antitrust laws . . . are the Magna Carta of free enterprise. They are as important to the preservation of economic freedom and our free enterprise system as the Bill of Rights is to the protection of our fundamental personal freedoms. And the freedom guaranteed each and every business, no matter how small, is the freedom to compete—to assert with vigor, imagination, devotion, and ingenuity whatever economic muscle it can muster.[50]

Traditionally, the antitrust laws have been applied only against private enterprise, and state action has typically been largely immunized against antitrust liability. But proponents of the market understand that the only barriers to entry and competition that can persist in the face of market forces are those erected or supported by government. Indeed, the black codes and early Jim Crow laws were based upon this very recognition.

In a series of decisions in the late 1970s and early 1980s, this realization prevailed upon a majority of the Supreme Court. Although unwilling to remove immunity from the states themselves, the Court narrowed the ability of cities to clothe themselves in state immunity. Declaring the antitrust laws "established a regime of competition as the fundamental principle governing commerce in this country,"[51] Justice Brennan concluded that cities could be liable whenever they placed "their own parochial interests above the nation's goals reflected in the antitrust laws."[52] This doctrine reached its pinnacle in *Community Communications Co. v. City of Boulder*,[53] in which the Court invalidated a municipal moratorium against cable television construction, holding that a state could only extend its antitrust immunity to local governments if it clearly articulated and actively supervised a policy designed to displace competition in the industry at issue. The *Boulder* decision provided a vehicle for entrepreneurs to challenge the pervasive monopoly privileges and protectionist regulations created by municipal fiefdoms through such mechanisms as franchising, licensing, and zoning, mechanisms that stifle opportunities in businesses spanning the spectrum from taxicabs to garbage collection and furniture moving.

This window of opportunity, however, was quickly slammed shut. Congress passed the Local Government Antitrust Act of 1984,[54] insulating municipalities from monetary damages for antitrust violations (although injunctions are still available). Moreover, the Supreme Court retrenched its *Boulder* doctrine in a pair of cases. In *Town of Hallie v. City of Eau Claire*,[55] the Court extended state immunity to municipalities whenever the state merely authorizes (rather than mandates) anticompetitive actions. Even more distressingly, the Court held in *Southern Motor Carriers Rate Conference v. United States*[56] that the state could extend its immunity to *private* price-fixing boards that enforce their will through the coercive power of the state. The Court thus substantially limited the availability of antitrust laws to challenge some of the most onerous and arbitrary deprivations of economic liberty. In so doing, the Court demonstrated the often fleeting nature of opportunities to vindicate civil rights. Perhaps if the civil rights movement had years ago established economic liberty as a top priority, created an effective network of legal advocacy organizations, and forcefully advocated judicial curbs against deprivations of economic liberty as a matter of civil rights, it could have prevailed in unleashing the antitrust laws against the source of the most invidious anticompetitive activity—government itself. Given the close division on the Court over these issues—and an indication that Justice Scalia may be sympathetic to applying antitrust laws to quasi-governmental actions[57]— advocates of civil rights should press forward with such efforts.

Yet another potentially fruitful theory by which to challenge regulatory excesses is advanced by Professor Epstein in *Takings*. The Constitution authorizes the government to take property for public use if due process and just compensation are provided. Proceeding from the natural rights theory of representative government that "the state's rights against its citizens are no greater than the sum of the rights of the individuals,"[58] Epstein reasons that the eminent domain power, restricted as it is by the public use and just compensation requirements, is validly exercised only where it leaves "individuals with rights more valuable than those they have been deprived of."[59] Thus, any "taking" of a person's property rights—real or personal wealth and the capacity to generate the same—is unconstitutional unless it satisfies this exacting standard. This theory can be applied to challenge involuntary transfer payments,[60] as well as any state-imposed dimunition in bargaining power. For instance, regulations that "cut to the heart of freedom of contract," such as wage and hour laws, could be challenged since they limit the ability of employers to dispose of their property and of employees to acquire property by use of their labor.[61]

These are but a few of the possible legal strategies that can be pursued in the cause of economic liberty. But more important than any particular strategy is the necessity of establishing the overall goal and resolving to attain it. Equal opportunity and the freedom to support one's life are vital components of civil rights, and they are endangered by those who exploit the power of the state to limit economic liberty. Without meaningful judicial scrutiny of such schemes, this vital component of our civil rights will remain at risk.

Expanding Educational Freedom

The liberty of individuals to secure an education free from state-created obstacles must also comprise a major focus of the legal strategy of a reinvigorated civil rights movement.

Educational freedom is hampered today in two principal ways. First, the coercive apparatus of the state is frequently invoked to standardize education and restrict parental discretion. Legal action can ensure maximum liberty for parents to act in the best interest of their children by choosing from the widest variety of educational alternatives their resources will allow them to pursue. Second, to the extent the state has undertaken to provide universal education, it has not made educational opportunities available on an equal basis. Legal action can assist in liberating poor and minority school children from the vice-grip of the public school monopoly and ensure equal educational opportunities.

The legal theory by which to achieve the first objective traces its roots, not surprisingly, to the same era of American jurisprudence in which economic liberty enjoyed maximum judicial protection. Unlike the *Lochner* doctrine, however, the principles of educational freedom have not been discarded by the Court—and in fact have been reaffirmed in recent years[62]—although they are rarely invoked in contemporary civil rights litigation.

Three cases during the mid-1920s form the great jurisprudential trilogy of educational liberty. In *Meyer v. Nebraska*, the Supreme Court struck down an "emergency" statute making it a criminal offense to teach any foreign language in public or private schools before the eighth grade. The Court overturned the conviction of a Lutheran school teacher who taught the German language through biblical stories, holding that the right of the instructor to teach and "the right of the parents to engage him so to instruct their children . . . are within the liberty of the [Fourteenth] Amendment."[63] Justice Holmes dissented, revealing the same antipathy toward educational freedom as he displayed toward economic liberty in his *Lochner* dissent, protesting that "it is desirable that all the citizens of the United States should speak a common tongue, and therefore . . . the end aimed at by the statute is a lawful and proper one."[64]

Four years later, the Court in *Farrington v. Tokushige* invalidated a law subjecting foreign language schools and their teachers in Hawaii to pervasive regulation. Among other restrictions, the statute required a permit from the Department of Instruction for the schools and their teachers; compelled the school's operator and teachers to pledge to "direct the minds and studies of pupils . . . to make them good and loyal American citizens, and . . . not permit such students to receive instructions in any way inconsistent therewith"; limited attendance to one hour per day; and authorized the department to prescribe textbooks and curricula.[65] The regulations were challenged by parents who desired to send their children to school to learn their ancestral Japanese language. The Court concluded the law violated the "fundamental rights of the individual,"[66] since "it would deprive parents of fair opportunity to procure for their children instruction which they think important and we cannot say is harmful."[67]

And in *Pierce v. Society of Sisters*, the Court struck down the ultimate barrier to educational freedom—a law forbidding education outside the public schools. Justice McReynolds declared that the statute "unreasonably interferes with the liberty of parents and guardians to direct the upbringing and education of children under their control."[68] The Court proclaimed,

> The fundamental theory of liberty upon which all governments in this Union repose excludes any general power of the State to standardize its children by forcing them to accept instruction from public teachers only. The child is not the mere creature of the State; those who nurture him and direct his destiny have the right, coupled with the high duty, to recognize and prepare him for additional obligations.[69]

These principles can be applied in two contemporary contexts. First, where private schools depart from conventional wisdom in their teaching methods or from predominant community values—or where the state attempts to regulate private schools out of existence through subtle yet onerous and arbitrary burdens—these principles may be applied to remove the yoke of the state. Such an approach would be particularly helpful to parents in those hundreds of private schools operated by and for poor and minority students for whom the traditional public school process failed. Second, these principles may be used to defend the right of conscientious parents to provide educational opportunities for their children as they see fit—including the tens of thousands of parents who educate their children at home. Far from assuming that such parents are criminals, as laws in many states purport to do, the emphasis should be on maximizing educational options, even if they do not reflect mainstream thought—which, to the extent it is characterized by the remarkable lack of success produced by the public education monopoly, is hardly a standard that should be emulated. A free society requires broad discretion for parents to act in the best interests of their children.

The second objective of the civil rights movement in this area must be equal educational opportunity. A great deal of progress was made through the desegregation mandate of *Brown v. Board of Education*; but as the preceding chapter demonstrates, the rampant social engineering of the past two decades has set back the quest for equal opportunity enormously. Clearly, a further reshuffling of students within the public school monopoly is unlikely to provide equal educational opportunity for those students who need and desire it the most. These students need some way out.

Some might advocate that those who have been victimized by deprivations of educational liberty should be preferentially advanced. But especially in the area of education, there can be no "short-cuts"; individuals who advance without achievement are being defrauded in the most pernicious way. Similarly, "proportional representation" schemes provide only a cosmetic change while leaving the underlying problems intact. Instead, the appropriate "remedy" for unequal educational opportunities is twofold: to remove barriers to educational opportunities, and to make those opportunities available on an equal basis.

The judicial mechanism to achieve these objectives is a "voucher" remedy for deprivations of equal educational opportunity, which would remove the principal impediment to such opportunity—the monopoly power of the public school system. Such deprivations are prevalent in at least two contexts. First, many school systems presently under court orders to achieve desegregation may engage in social engineering for decades without accomplishing desegregation or providing equal educational opportunities. Students are the pawns in these ongoing machinations, and their only hope for educational opportunity is to escape the system. Second, many school systems are nominally desegregated, but are engaging in a new form of discrimination—in essence, a kind of intra-school segregation, taking the form of a two-track system in which poor and minority students are "steered away" from certain educational offerings, or are held to lower standards.[70] These differential standards are based on the tacit assumption that some students, because of their ethnic background, are incapable of or unsuited for rigorous academic programs, an assumption that is inevitably self-fulfilling and profoundly debilitating.

An appropriate remedy in either type of case would be damages under 42 U.S.C. § 1983, based upon the right to equal protection under the Fourteenth Amendment and the substantive right to non-discrimination in education under Title IV of the Civil Rights Act of 1964. The damages would be equal to the student's share of state per-pupil expenditures, in the form of a voucher that could be applied against tuition at a public or private school that would fulfil the right to equal opportunity.[71]

Unlike failed solutions such as busing, a voucher remedy would not violate the civil rights of innocent individuals but would effectively cure the deprivation of the victim's civil rights. Widespread application of this strategy would produce two positive consequences. First, it would release the most disadvantaged students from the shackles of failed public schools, and enable them to apply the funds allocated for their education to a positive use. Second, it would encourage public school districts to concentrate on education rather than social engineering. In the long run, any degree of long overdue competition infused into education may well operate to improve and strengthen public education; but in any event, it will certainly reduce the barriers that poor and minority children must now overcome to pursue any meaningful educational opportunities at all.

A voucher-type opt-out remedy was recently provided in a different but analogous context. A group of parents sued the Hawkins County, Tennessee, school district, which had suspended their children for refusing to read certain textbooks that offended their religious beliefs. Rather than seeking to ban the offensive textbooks, the parents successfully sought reimbursement for tuition incurred at the private and public schools that accomodated the children.[72] The notion that parents who object to the orthodoxy of the public educational orthodoxy should not only be able to remove their children but take their tax money with them is fully consistent with the principles of a free society. Such remedies offer enormous potential for vindicating civil rights.

Voucher remedies have not yet been tested in the civil rights context, and such efforts could require dozens of attempts before success. But the civil rights movement—at least until recent years—has never lacked in creativity, tenacity, or resolve. The magnitude of the deprivations of educational freedom that exist today—and the tragic ramifications resulting from them—commend this area for special attention by a reinvigorated civil rights movement in the years ahead.

Civil Rights, Natural Rights

Many advocates of civil rights are reluctant to use legal mechanisms such as antitrust laws and the Civil Rights Act because they have been misapplied in the past, and such hesitancy is understandable. But given the retreat of the judiciary from its assigned role under the Constitution as the principal defender of fundamental rights, and given that the judiciary is the only branch of government capable of safeguarding individual rights, advocates of civil rights must use every legitimate means at their disposal to induce the judiciary to assume that role. And where necessary, i.e., where constitutional arguments are unlikely to prevail in a hostile judicial climate, such efforts should include creative legal strategies such as the statutory approaches outlined herein. To the extent that the antitrust laws can be applied to safeguard entrepreneurial freedom, or that the Civil Rights Act—or any other law—can provide protection for individual liberty, they should be aggressively applied to further those ends, until it is once again possible to assert fundamental rights in and of themselves.

Similarly, those who occupy the front lines in the legal battle for civil rights must remain ever-mindful that such rights, in their essence, are conferred by no statute, but are in reality rights that are retained by the people in a free society, as proclaimed in the Declaration of Independence and safeguarded by the Constitution. Thus, advocates of civil rights should always accompany narrow, legalistic arguments with an exposition of the broader, fundamental nature of the civil rights asserted. Over time, if only by increment, the terms of the debate shall be altered, the moral high ground reclaimed, and the quest for civil rights restored to its proper course.

Notes

1. See, e.g., Clint Bolick, "A Call to Judicial Action," *Lincoln Review* (Spring 1983), p. 49-55.
2. Antonin Scalia, "On the Merits of the Frying Pan," *Regulation* (January/February 1985), p. 10. The conference was a program of the Cato Instutute.
3. Id., p. 12.
4. Id.
5. Richard A. Epstein, "The Active Virtues," *Regulation* (January/February 1985), p. 16.
6. Siegan, p. 6.
7. Terry Eastland, "'We Are All Activists Now,'" *Wall Street Journal* (Oct. 31, 1985), p. 30.
8. Richard A. Epstein, *Takings* (Cambridge, MA: Harvard University Press, 1985), p. 31.

9. Stephen Macedo, *The New Right and the Constitution* (Washington, D.C.: Cato Institute, 1986), p. 27.

10. Id., p. 24-25.

11. Id., p. 26.

12. Alexander Hamilton, "No. 78," in Hamilton, John Jay, and James Madison, *The Federalist* (New York: The Modern American Library, 1941), p. 508.

13. Id., p. 506.

14. Id., p. 508.

15. Id., p. 509-10.

16. Id., p. 503.

17. Id., p. 505.

18. Id., p. 505-06.

19. *Marbury v. Madison*, 5 U.S. 137, 163 (1803).

20. Id., p. 177.

21. Hamilton, p. 504.

22. *Slaughter-House Cases*, p. 105 (Field, J., dissenting).

23. Id., p. 110.

24. Id., p. 116 (Bradley, J., dissenting).

25. *Yick Wo v. Hopkins*, 118 U.S. 356, 366 (1886).

26. Id., p. 368.

27. Id., p. 373-74.

28. Id., p. 370.

29. *Lochner v. New York*, 198 U.S. 45, 64 (1905).

30. Id., p. 52-53.

31. Id., p. 61-62.

32. Id., p. 57.

33. Justice Holmes is revered by many as a great jurist, but the reasons for such historical stature escape this author. His opinions, like his dissent in *Lochner*, reveal a remarkably authoritarian tendency. See, e.g., *Davis v. Massachusetts*, 167 U.S. 43 (1897), affirming the conviction of a preacher for making a speech in the Boston Common without a permit; *Patterson v. Colorado*, 205 U.S. 454 (1907), upholding the conviction of a cartoonist for satirizing the Colorado Supreme Court; and *Block v. Hirsh*, 256 U.S. 134 (1921), sustaining the suspension of private property rights of landlords during World War I.

34. *Lochner*, p. 75 (Holmes, J., dissenting).

35. Id., p. 76.

36. Id., p. 77.

37. Id., p. 75.

38. "Crisis in the Courts," *Manhattan Report on Economic Policy*, vol. V, no. 2 (1982), p. 4.

39. *Williamson v. Lee Optical*, 348 U.S. 483, 487 (1955).

40. Id., p. 488.

41. *City of New Orleans v. Dukes*, 427 U.S. 297, 303 (1976).

42. *New State Ice Co. v. Liebmann*, 285 U.S. 262 (1932).

43. For a discussion of these cases and their potential significance, see David O. Stewart, "A growing equal protection clause?" *ABA Journal* (October 1985), p. 108-20. Unlike many of the cases decided in the *Lochner* era, which were decided under the "liberty" clause of the Fourteenth Amendment, these cases—*City of Cleburne v. Cleburne Living Center*, 105 S. Ct. 3249 (1985); *Metropolitan Life Insurance Co. v. Ward*, 105 S. Ct. 1676 (1985); and *Williams*

v. Vermont, 105 S. Ct. 2465 (1985)—were decided under the equal protection clause.

44. *Monnell v. Department of Social Services*, 436 U.S. 658 (1978).
45. *Washington v. Davis*, 426 U.S. 229, 239-40 (1976).
46. *United States v. Town of Cicero*, 786 F.2d 331, 334 (7th Cir. 1986)(Posner, J., concurring and dissenting).
47. Id., p. D-2.
48. *Puntolillo v. New Hampshire Racing Commission*, 375 F. Supp. 1089, 1090 (D.N.H. 1974). See also *Sibley Memorial Hospital v. Wilson*, 488 F.2d 1338 (D.C. Cir. 1973).
49. See Clint Bolick, "Use Antitrust Law Against Local Government Offenders," *Wall Street Journal* (August 16, 1984), p. 22.
50. *U.S. v. Topco Associates*, 405 U.S. 596, 610 (1972).
51. *Lafayette v. Louisiana Power & Light Co.*, 435 U.S. 389, 398 (1978).
52. Id., p. 413.
53. *Community Communications Co. v. City of Boulder*, 455 U.S. 40 (1982).
54. Public Law No. 98-544 (1984).
55. *Town of Hallie v. City of Eau Claire*, 105 S. Ct. 1713 (1985).
56. *Southern Motor Carriers Rate Conference v. United States*, 105 S. Ct. 1721 (1985).
57. In *324 Liquor Corp. v. Duffy*, 55 U.S.L.W. 4094 (U.S. Jan. 13, 1987), the Supreme Court invalidated as an antitrust violation a New York law requiring minimum liquor prices enforced by a private board backed by the authority of the state.
58. Epstein, *Takings*, p. 331.
59. Id., p. 332.
60. Id., p. 314-24.
61. Id., p. 280.
62. See, e.g., *Wisconsin v. Yoder*, 406 U.S. 205, 213-14 (1972).
63. *Meyer v. Nebraska*, 262 U.S. 390, 400 (1923).
64. *Bartels v. Iowa*, 262 U.S. 404, 412 (1923)(Holmes, J., dissenting).
65. *Farrington v. Tokushige*, 273 U.S. 284, 293-94 (1927).
66. Id., p. 299.
67. Id., p. 298.
68. *Pierce v. Society of Sisters*, 268 U.S. 510, 534-35 (1925).
69. Id., p. 535.
70. See, e.g., *United States v. Yonkers Board of Education*, 624 F. Supp. 1276, 1528 (S.D.N.Y. 1985). See also Gene I. Maeroff, "School Standards: U.S. Inquiry on Minorities Draws Suspicion," *New York Times* (Sept. 24, 1985), p. A18.
71. The author is indebted to Professor John Coons of the School of Law of the University of California at Berkeley for suggesting a variation of this approach.
72. *Mozert v. Hawkins County Public Schools*, 647 F. Supp. 1194 (E.D. Tenn. 1986); and slip op. (E.D. Tenn. Dec. 18, 1986).

8

The Prognosis for Success

The task presently confronting advocates of civil rights is one of restoration and refinement. Restoration, because the principles of civil rights have been confused and distorted, and the consensus that produced the great triumphs of civil rights has been eroded. Refinement, because the core principles of civil rights have been established in the law of the land, and need only to be applied to the remaining deprivations of civil rights—the contradictions between the vision and the reality—that exist today.

Given the largely unchallenged dominance of the civil rights establishment, the prognosis for moving forward is mixed, but there are some bright lights on the horizon. Perhaps the most hopeful sign is a relaxation of the suppression of dissenting views by the civil rights establishment, along with a growing recognition that its agenda has failed. The 1986 convention of the National Urban League in San Francisco, for instance, featured such speakers as Governor Thomas Kean of New Jersey, who evoked broad agreement when he charged that "the same government that gave civil rights to black Americans [has] too often asked for dependency in return."[1] Thus could columnist William Raspberry recently observe,

> For a couple of years now, it has been all right for black leaders to talk about family disintegration as a source of some of the problems facing black America. More recently, the idea has gained acceptability that black people themselves, not just the government, must take a share of the responsibility for setting things right.[2]

Echoes Urban League President John Jacob, "For too long we have pinned our hopes on good white people or the government to solve our problems," and "have been defensive about problems within our own communities that we should be tackling ourselves."[3] Indeed, the Urban League has committed substantial resources to programs designed to reduce crime and prevent one-parent families.[4]

This resurgent emphasis on self-help has been accompanied by some reconsideration of the civil rights establishment's policies. Raspberry declares,

> We have rediscovered truths so obvious that we wonder how we ever lost touch with them: that work is the only noncorrosive means of gaining income (at least for the poor); that you cannot remove the sting of charity without also removing the incentive to independence; that you cannot produce industry by rewarding sloth.[5]

Yet this re-evaluation does not extend to all among the civil rights establishment; and even such a relatively moderate organization as the National Urban League, though it supports enterprise zone legislation, continues to advocate preferential treatment and oppose educational vouchers and the elimination of the minimum wage.[6]

Along the civil rights establishment's critical self-analysis, Urban League president Jacob observes that "new voices are being heard from Black America, new voices that are raising questions about policies and approaches toward solving problems that afflict this community," and whose emergence is neither "surprising nor unwelcome."[7] The rise of new black leaders is vitally important to the cause of civil rights since blacks are still disproportionately disadvantaged by civil rights deprivations. These new black leaders, spanning the range from moderate to conservative to libertarian, may not all endorse the back to basics approach outlined in this book or completely renounce the revisionists' political agenda, but all exhibit a refreshing willingness to take independent positions and consider alternatives. Among others, this new generation includes scholars such as Glenn Loury, Thomas Sowell, Walter Williams, and Ann Wortham; activists such as Marva Collins, Robert Woodson, Jay Parker, and Joan Davis Ratteray; public servants such as Clarence Thomas, William Lucas, and L. Douglas Wilder; and journalists such as William Raspberry, Lawrence Wade, and Joseph Perkins. Their influence will surely grow as the quest for civil rights is restored to its original course.

Equally significant is the burgeoning awareness among some white conservatives that civil rights are important and that positive policy alternatives premised upon individual liberty and free enterprise must be developed. At the forefront of this effort are Education Secretary William Bennett; EEOC Vice Chairman Rosalie Silberman; Assistant Attorney General William Bradford Reynolds; former Delaware governor Pete duPont; Representatives Jack Kemp, Vin Weber, Newt Gingrich, James Courter, and the Conservative Opportunity Society; Manhattan Institute President William Hammett; Virginia Thomas of the U.S. Chamber of

Commerce; Michael Kennedy of the Associated General Contractors; and Jeffrey Zuckerman, Director of the Bureau of Competition at the Federal Trade Commission. Perhaps there is enough potential statesmanship and common ground to produce a new direction for civil rights in America's third century.

To do so, we must take stock of where we are and where we need to go. One view is provided by William Raspberry, who recently proclaimed that "the Civil Rights Movement is over." By civil rights, Raspberry referred to "institutionalized access to the basic opportunities a society owes its citizens . . . because they are citizens"—in essence, "the right to compete." The battle for civil rights, he argued, is essentially won; thus, the challenge confronting blacks has "less to do with base-line opportunity than with efforts to transform that opportunity into concrete results." But while "society can distribute opportunity," Raspberry declared, "it cannot distribute victories." He attributed much of the confusion on this point to "mislabeling"—"our insistence on describing every racial shortfall as an abridgement of civil rights." He explained that "when we apply the term 'civil rights'" to those political leaders who represent the special needs and interests of blacks, "it tempts us to think in terms of distribution and enforcement when we ought to be thinking of discipline and exertion." Thus, he concluded "[e]nforcement of civil rights can ensure us only a place in the starting gate. What is required for victory is that we run like hell."[8]

Raspberry's analysis is powerful and perceptive. But it would be unfortunate to infer that no place exists for a civil rights movement today. As long as barriers to economic opportunity and economic liberty persist—as long as a cycle of government-enforced dependency exists—serious civil rights issues remain. This is true even if these impediments to civil rights are not drawn on the basis of race, for like all such impediments, they deny those outside the mainstream the fundamental guarantees of a free society.

Once the movement is restored, the real challenges will begin. The political climate is generally favorable for both economic and educational liberty; but powerful interests who benefit from the status quo, such as labor unions, will block progress wherever possible. And while the composition of the federal judiciary has changed dramatically in recent years, many of the new judges may be receptive to individual liberty as a policy matter but hesitant to fulfill their constitutional role in safeguarding that liberty due to an overly broad conception of "judicial restraint." Thus, as in the past, the quest for civil rights will require tenacity, creativity, and fidelity to basic principles.

The one problem area with the greatest prospect for progress is the cycle of poverty. Greater consensus exists over this civil rights issue than with any other. But this quagmire is chronic and systemic, and we must resist short-term, quick-fix solutions. More than any other, the dependency problem requires statesmenship, not polemics.

Such a prescription, of course, applies to all issues of civil rights, for the civil rights mission is central to the moral legitimacy of this nation. At bottom, the prognosis for a renaissance of the civil rights movement is positive; for the quest for civil rights simply *must* progress, lest we surrender the legacy that makes ours a nation of freedom.

Notes

1. Joseph Perkins, "Urban League Emphasizes an Agenda of Self-Help," *Wall Street Journal* (August 6, 1986), p. 16.
2. William Raspberry, "Black Criminals, Black Victims," *Washington Post* (October 31, 1985), p. A21.
3. Jacob, "New Realities," p. 255.
4. Perkins, p. 16.
5. William Raspberry, "Welfare—By Any Other Name," *Washington Post* (November 13, 1985), p. A21.
6. See, e.g., John E. Jacob, "An Overview of Black America in 1985," p. x; and James Williams, p. 178-81.
7. Jacob, "Overview," p. x.
8. William Raspberry, "The Civil Rights Movement Is Over," *Washington Post* (February 25, 1987), p. A23.

Conclusion

We have the power to begin the world over again.

—Thomas Paine

The words above were first uttered by a passionate advocate of civil rights at the commencement of a nation dedicated to the ideals of fundamental individual rights and equality under the law. They were repeated two centuries later by another great civil rights advocate, Martin Luther King, at the apex of triumph for those ideals.[1]

The 200 years between Paine and King were years of challenge and extraordinary change, both evolutionary and revolutionary. The one constant throughout, however, was the existence of a movement characterized by an unwavering commitment to the original principles of civil rights, a commitment that has been abandoned by many of those who today hold themselves out as civil rights leaders. For that reason, substantial cause for concern exists over whether the ideals of civil rights—the ideals that support America's claim to moral supremacy and set it apart from authoritarian regimes around the world—can endure this challenge. Certainly these ideals cannot prevail if they are not championed by those who cherish them.

This book, along with a few others written in recent years, is contrary to a prevailing orthodoxy whose purveyors stifle debate and dissent through derision, quarantine, and character assassination. The time when such a reactionary response is possible, however, is quickly coming to an end, for the architects of the revised civil rights agenda are being called to account for the effects of their policies, which have polarized Americans and thwarted opportunities for poor and minority individuals to gain their share of the American Dream. Indeed, the revisionists have not only declined to address the three major civil rights issues today—entrepreneurial opportunities, educational liberty, and the vicious cycle of poverty—but in fact their policies have exacerbated these problems.

Nonetheless, this book is not intended to impugn the integrity of the contemporary civil rights establishment. No doubt, many of its leaders are sincere in their beliefs, and their past bona fide contributions to the cause of civil rights cannot be ignored. But by abandoning the core principles of civil rights, they have relinquished their claim to leadership in the quest for civil rights.

But whatever their motivations, whatever the implications of their actions, the revisionists will retain their erroneous identification with civil rights for as long as they are allowed to define the terms of the debate. To redefine those terms, we must take a careful look at exactly what is happening. Reduced to its essence, the battle now is between statism and liberty. The term "statism" is not fully adequate, since the revisionists do not seek an enlargement of the state as an end in itself; but it is descriptive in that at the core of the revised agenda is the coercive apparatus of the state—not to guarantee civil rights, but to redistribute wealth and power. Before any civil rights movement can make progress in America's third century, the concept of civil rights must be restored to the universally understood meaning that preceded the revised agenda—that is, civil rights are those fundamental individual rights that we all hold equally as Americans.

Beyond that, sincere advocates of this ideal must identify the most critical obstacles to civil rights and craft an effective strategy to overcome them, premised on the principles that inspired the movement for its first two centuries. This book describes the most obvious obstacles and offers some possible solutions; but success will ultimately be attained only if the civil rights movement can call upon the same ingenuity and commitment exhibited by its past heroes, from Frederick Douglass and William Lloyd Garrison to Booker T. Washington and Martin Luther King. It is the vision of these heroes that the present movement has abandoned—and which the new civil rights leaders must reclaim.

One final note. In discussing my ideas for this book with some prospective sponsors and publishers, a common reaction was that such ideas could more plausibly be presented by a black person. That such a remark can be made is a sad commentary on the state of civil rights today. The tragic legacy of the misdirected civil rights agenda during the past two decades is that many people now seem to believe that one's interest in civil rights— and the legitimacy of one's opinions on such issues—is somehow related to skin color. If that is an accurate assessment, we have accomplished little in the past two centuries. If nothing else, the advocates of civil rights must make it plain that *every* individual has an equal, personal, and vital interest in civil rights.

This book, then, is not—indeed, cannot—be addressed solely to whites, or to blacks. The principles set forth herein have been forcefully advocated by men and women of every color, and they must continue to be, if the quest for civil rights can have any chance to succeed. The challenge is for whites to learn the lessons of the past two decades; for blacks, to demand and exploit the opportunities that America's commitment to civil rights is intended to guarantee; and for all Americans, to be faithful to the ideals upon which this nation's claim to greatness is based.

Note

1. King, *Where Do We Go from Here: Chaos or Community?*, p. 71.

Index

Abolition movement: and Republican Party, 22; and Revolutionary leaders, 14, 18; demise of, 27–28; legacy of, 27–28; origins of, 14, 18
Abram, Morris, 48, 57, 60, 75
Acton, Lord, 5
Adams, John Quincy, 19
Affirmative action, 63–75, 86–88, 90
"American Creed," 13, 40–41, 84
American Revolution, 9–10
Anti-Defamation League, 66
Antitrust, 133–34, 139

Bakke, 66–71, 123
"benign" discrimination, 25
Berea College v. Kentucky, 37, 44
Berry, Mary Frances, 58
Birney, James, 20–21
Black codes, 25, 32–33
Blackmun, Harry, 67–69, 71
Blackstone, Sir William, 13
Bratton v. City of Detroit, 69–70
Brennan, William, 61, 66, 68–69, 71, 73, 133
Brown, John, 22
Brown v. Bd. of Education, 44–45, 60, 62, 65, 72, 74, 104, 105, 122–23, 137
Bunzel, John, 83
Busing, 60–63, 138

Carmichael, Stokely, 46
Carter, Jimmy, 85–86, 98
Cassell v. State of Texas, 43–44
Civil rights: contemporary deprivations of, xiii, 93–118, 146; defined, xi–xii, 6–11, 17, 42, 144; revised definition, 55–59, 74–75, 147. *See also* Civil Rights Movement
Civil Rights Act of 1866, 25–26
Civil Rights Act of 1871, 27
Civil Rights Act of 1964, 48–49, 64–65, 71, 73, 132–33, 138, 139

Civil rights establishment: agenda of, xi, 55–60, 74–75, 82–90, 147; and black opinion, 90, 110; and forced busing, 60–63; and racial preferences, 63–75, 82–83, 86–88, 90; and redistribution of wealth, 56, 60, 82, 84–87, 89; authoritarianism of, 59, 89–90; failure of, 82–90; ideological tenets of, 55–60, 74–75; origins of, 53–55; use of political power, 55, 75, 89; views of education, 56
Civil rights movement: agenda of modern movement, xi, 55–60, 74–75, 82–90, 147; and Booker T. Washington, 33–36; and World War II, 41–43; classical versus separatist, 38–39, 46–47, 54–55; during 1950s-60s, 43–49; Niagra movement, 39; origins of, 3, 5, 39; split between DuBois and Garvey, 38–39; transformation during 1960s, xi, 4, 53–60
Civil War, 24, 31
City of New Orleans v. Dukes, 130–31
Collectivism. *See* Group rights
Color-blindness, xii, 26–27, 36–37, 40–49, 57, 58, 65, 68, 70, 74, 123
Community Communications Co. v. City of Boulder, 133–34
Constitution: and proper role of judiciary, 123–27, 139; and slavery, 16–17, 21–23; Art. I, section 2, 16–17; Art. 1, section 9, 16; color-blindness, *See* separate heading; Fifteenth Amendment, 27; Fifth Amendment, 26; Fourteenth Amendment, *See* separate heading; Ninth Amendment, 16, 125; "privileges or immunities" cause, *See Slaughter-House Cases*; slave compromise, 16–17; "takings" clause, 134–35; Tenth Amendment, 16, 125; Thirteenth Amendment, 24; Twenty-fourth Amendment, 48
Crime, 116–18
"Crisis of victory," 17–18, 32, 75, 81–83

Cycle of poverty, 112–18, 144–45

Davis-Bacon Act, 101–02
Declaration of Independence, 10–11, 14–15, 22–23, 38, 45–46, 128, 139
Declaration of the Rights of Man, 9
DeFunis v. Odegaard, 65–66
Depression, 40
de Tocqueville, Alexis, 8
Discrimination: changing meaning of, 58–59, 68
Dorsey, Stuart, 98–99
Douglass, Frederick, xxi, 20, 21, 24, 27, 31–34, 89
Douglas, Stephen, 23
Douglas, William O., 65–66, 70, 130
Dred Scott v. Sandford, 21–22, 23, 27, 36, 65, 122
Drug laws, 117–18
DuBois, W.E.B., xii, 34, 35, 38–39, 116

Eastland, Terry, 125
Economic liberty: and Civil Rights Act of 1964, 48–49; as a civil right, 32, 95, 131; barriers to, 48, 49, 93–104; judicial action to promote, 123–24, 127–35, nullified in post-Civil War era, 25, 32–33, 97, proposed Economic Liberty Act, 100, 103
Education: and black achievement, 86; and equal opportunity, 45–47, 86, 104–6, 137–38; and forced busing, 60–63, 112, 138; and private schools, 107–12, 136–37; and public school monopoly, 104–12; barrriers to opportunities, 93, 104–8; civil rights establishment's view of, 56; during Jim Crow era, 35; judicial action to promote opportunity, 135–38; of slaves, 18–19; tuition tax credits, 110–12; vouchers, 110–12, 137–38
Emerson, Ralph Waldo, 31
Enterprise zones, 103–04
Entrepreneurial opportunities, *See* Economic liberty
Epstein, Richard, 124–25, 134–35
Equality: definition of, 9–10; Lincoln's view of, 22–23; moral equality, 22–23; of opportunity, 9, 43–44, 47, 49, 59; of outcome, *See also* Preferential treatment, 9–10, 54–60, 62, 68–69, 74, 82, 84–89;

of rights, 7–10, 19, 26–27, 36–37, 54; shift in definition during 1960s, 54–60; under law, 26–27, 36–37, 67, 74; versus liberty, 9–10, 92–93
Equal protection, *See* Fourteenth Amendment
Executive Order 11246, 63

Families (black), 85, 142
Farmer, James, 47
Farrakhan, Louis, 89–90
Farrington v. Tokushige, 136
Federalist No. 78, 126
Field, Stephen, 32, 128
Fifteenth Amendment, 27
Fifth Amendment, 26
Firefighters v. Stotts, 71
Fitzhugh, George, 24–25
Fourteenth Amendment, 26, 32, 37, 43–45, 48, 65–72, 128–32, 136, 138
Frankfurter, Felix, 43–44
Freedmen Acts, 24
Free enterprise, *See* Economic liberty
Free Soil Party, 21–22
Fried, Charles, 130
Friedman, Milton, 95, 106, 107, 117
Fugitive Slave Law, 21–22, 24

Garrison, William Lloyd, 20–21, 27, 31, 89
Garvey, Marcus, 39
Glazer, Nathan, 55, 57, 62–63, 74–75
Great Society, 85, 113, 116
Green v. County School Board of New Kent County, 61
Griggs v. Duke Power Co., 63–65
Group rights, 57–58, see also Quotas

Hamilton, Alexander, 125–27
Hammond, Ray, 105
Harlan, John M., 36–37, 73, 123
Harrington, Michael, 56, 59
Hayek, F.A., 9–10, 17
Henry, Patrick, 16
Higgs, Robert, 33
Hitler, Adolph, 40, 42, 46
Holmes, Oliver Wendell, 129–30, 136
Hooks, Benjamin, 58, 83
Howard, Jeff, 105
Humphrey, Hubert, 48–49

Income, black versus white, 82, 85–87, 105
Individual rights, 6, 46–47, 49, 57, 67–68, 93

Jackson, Andrew, 19
Jackson, Jesse, 58, 68, 89
Jackson, Robert, 41–42
Jacob, John E., 60, 89, 142–43
Japanese internment, 41
Jefferson, Thomas, 6, 10, 14–15, 47
Jencks, Christopher, 56, 105
Jim Crow laws, 25, 32–33, 35–37, 95, 97, 132–33
Johnson, Andrew, 24, 26
Johnson, Lyndon, 57, 63. *See also* Great Society
Johnson v. Transportation Agency, 72–74
Jones, Nathaniel, 69
Jordan, Winthrop, 14, 54
Judicial branch, role in protecting civil rights, 122–39

Kennedy, John, 47–48, 54
Keyes v. School District No. 1, 61
King, Martin Luther, xii, 5, 10, 13, 45–47, 54, 68, 116, 146
Korematsu v. United States, 41–42, 65
Krauthammer, Charles, 65

"law of nature," 5–6
Leadership Conference for Civil Rights, 123n
Liberty versus equality, 9–10, 40, 43–44, 47
Licensing, *See* Occupational licensing laws
Lincoln, Abraham, xii, 22–24
Local Government Antitrust Act of 1984, 134
Lochner v. New York, 129–30, 131, 135
Locke, John, 5–6
Loury, Glenn, 58, 88, 108, 116, 143

Macedo, Stephen, 125
Madison, James, 125
Malcolm X, 46
Marbury v. Madison, 127
Marshall, John, 127
Marshall, Thurgood, 44, 61, 65–69, 133
Marsh, Stuart, 69–72, 74
Marsh v. Board of Education, 69–72
McLaurin v. Oklahoma State Regents, 44

McPherson, James M., 18, 32
Meyer v. Nebraska, 135–36
Milliken v. Bradley, 61
Minimum wage, 49, 100–3
Monopolies, 32, 99–100, 128, 133–34
Mozert v. Hawkins County Public Schools, 138
Mueller v. Allen, 111–12
Murray, Charles, 55, 85–86, 105, 113–17
Myrdal, Gunnar, 13, 14, 34–35, 40–41, 42, 84, 105

National Association for the Advancement of Colored People (NAACP): and color-blindness, 40, 44–45, 46, 58; modern agenda, 83; original program, 40; origins of, 39–40. *See also* Civil rights establishment
National Urban League, 60, 89, 110, 142–43. *See also* Civil rights establishment
natural law, 5–11, 44–45
natural rights, 5–11, 14
Newblatt, Stuart, 70–72
Niagra movement, 39
Ninth Amendment, 16, 125

Occupational licensing laws, 25, 96–100, 132–33

Paine, Thomas, 3, 5–11, 18, 65, 81, 126, 146
Parks, Rosa, 45, 70
Pendleton, Clarence, 62, 89
Pierce, Samuel, 104
Pierce v. Society of Sisters, 136
Phillips, Wendell, 24
Plessy v. Ferguson, 36–37, 43, 45, 57, 65, 69, 74, 122–23
Poverty, 85–87, 94, 112–18, 144–45
Powell, Lewis, 67–69, 72
Preferential treatment, 63–75, 82–83, 86–88, 90
Private schools, 108–12
"privileges or immunities" clause. *See Slaughter-House Cases*

Quotas, 48, 63–75, 82–83, 86–88, 90

Radical Republicans, 24–27
Randolph, A. Philip, 42
Raspberry, William, 61, 88, 142–44

Reagan, Ronald, 86, 90, 113–15
Reconstruction, 24–28, 31
Redistribution of wealth, 56, 60, 82, 84–87, 89
Regents of the University of California v. Bakke, 66–71, 123
Rehnquist, William, 67, 73, 112
Reparations, 56
Republican Party, 22, 43
Reverse discrimination, 63–75, 82–83, 86–88, 90
Revisionists. *See* Civil rights establishment
Revolutionary War, 9–10
Reynolds, Wm. Bradford, 89
Rights. *See* Civil rights; Group rights; Individual rights; Natural rights
Rights of Man, 6–10
Roback, Jennifer, 33, 95
Roosevelt, Franklin D., 40–42, 112, 130
Rottenberg, Simon, 49, 101–02
Rustin, Bayard, 49, 53, 55

Scalia, Antonin, 73, 124, 134
segregation, 37, 60–63, 137–38
self-help, 142–43
"separate but equal," 36–43
separatism, 38–39, 46–47, 54–55
Shenefield, John H., 98
Siegan, Bernard, 125
Silberman, Rosalie (Ricky), ix, 143
Slaughter-House Cases, 32, 49, 97, 122–23, 128
Slavery: abolished, 24; and capitalism, 14, 17; and education, 18–19; and manumission, 18; and private property, 18; compromise on, at Constitutional Convention, 16–17; incompatability with civil rights, 13–15, 19–20, 22–23; justification of, 15–17, 23
Smith, Adam, 14
Smith, James P., 85–86
social contract, 6–7, 15–16
Sowell, Thomas, 93, 105
Spangler v. Pasadena Board of Education, 61

Southern Motor Carriers Rate Conference v. United States, 134
Stephens, Alexander, 23
Stevens, Thaddeus, 26
Stewart, Potter, 67
Stotts, 71
Sumner, Charles, 19
Swann v. Charlotte-Mecklenburg Board of Education, 61

"Takings" clause, 134–35
Taney, Roger, 22–23
Tappan, Lewis, 19–20
Tenth Amendment, 16, 125
Thirteenth Amendment, 24
Thomas, Clarence, ix, 63, 89–90, 143
Title VII. *See* Civil Rights Act of 1964
To Secure These Rights, 42–43
Town of Hallie v. City of Eau Claire, 134
Truman, Harry, 42–43, 117
Tuition tax credits, 110–12
Turner, Nat, 19

United States v. Town of Cicero, 132

Vietnam War, 54
Voting rights, 27, 32–33
Vouchers (education), 110–12, 137–38

Washington, Booker T., xii, 33–39, 116
Welch, Finis, 85–86
Welfare, 40, 85–86, 112–16
White, Byron, 66, 68–69, 71, 73
Wilkins, Roy, 46
Williams, Walter, 59, 87, 95–96, 99, 111
Williamson v. Lee Optical, 130
Wilson, James, 26
Wilson, Woodrow, 40
World War II, 41
Wortham, Anne, 55–56, 74–75
Wygant v. Jackson Bd. of Education, 72, 74, 123

Yick Wo v. Hopkins, 128–29
Young, Whitney, 59, 116